PRELUDE TO COURAGE

An Air Warrior's Journey of Faith

David H. Bergquist

HERITAGE BOOKS
2011

HERITAGE BOOKS
AN IMPRINT OF HERITAGE BOOKS, INC.

Books, CDs, and more—Worldwide

For our listing of thousands of titles see our website at
www.HeritageBooks.com

Published 2011 by
HERITAGE BOOKS, INC.
Publishing Division
100 Railroad Ave. #104
Westminster, Maryland 21157

Copyright © 2011 David H. Bergquist

The portrait on the cover is from a charcoal sketch done of Austin Keith by his navigatior, Milton Smith, in 1944.

All rights reserved. No part of this book may be reproduced or transmitted in any form or by any means, electronic or mechanical, including photocopying, recording or by any information storage and retrieval system without written permission from the author, except for the inclusion of brief quotations in a review.

International Standard Book Numbers
Paperbound: 978-0-7884-5356-4
Clothbound: 978-0-7884-8900-6

Lt. William H. A. Anderson

Dedication

To William H. A. Anderson, my uncle, and to all who flew in the United States Army Air Forces during World War II

Contents

List of Illustrations	*vii*
Acknowledgements	*ix*
Prologue	*xi*
1. Tokyo Bound	*1*
2. He Loved to Play a Part	*11*
3. Too Quickly Passed These Days	*22*
4. Up, Up, and Away	*31*
5. More of the Same	*43*
6. The Play	*53*
7. A Constant Guiding Star	*66*
8. The Letter	*83*
9. Abide with Me, Fast Falls the Eventide	*94*
10. At 10 Boynton Street: Cum Magno Me Delore	*99*
Epilogue	*116*
Notes	*123*
Bibliography	*135*
Index	*139*

Illustrations

Portrait of Austin Keith.............Author's Collection...................................... *cover*
Lt. William H.A. Anderson.......Author's Collection........................*facing page iii*
Nancy Marcoux..........................Author's Collection.........................*facing page ix*

Chapter One

Ponderous Peg Being Readied
for a Mission...........................National Archives...........................*facing page 3*
The Crew at Clovis
Army Air Field, Fall 1944......Peter B. Seel....................................*facing page 5*
The B-29 Cockpit....................National Museum of USAF..............*facing page 7*
The Crew at Saipan,
January 1945............................Author's Collection..........................*facing page 9*
The Ghastly Goose Nose Art by
Lt. Milt Smith, Navigator.......Author's Collection.......................*facing page 11*

Chapter Two

10 Boynton Street, Bangor.....Author's Collection........................*facing page 13*
Austin at 10..............................Author's Collection........................*facing page 15*
Illustration from
"I'll Take Basketball"..............*Oracle*, December 1936..................*facing page 17*
The Officers' Club..................Author's Collection........................*facing page 19*
Souvenir Scabbard
and Blade.......................Courtesy of Bette Barker Taverner..........*facing page 21*

Chapter Three

Football Cheering Squad,
1940...............................1942 Prism, University of Maine............*facing page 23*
Austin as
Rozencrantz.........Bricker Collection, Fogler Library, U. of M. ....*facing page 25*
Ozzie as Nat Miller................Author's Collection........................*facing page 27*
Austin as Johnny....................Author's Collection........................*facing page 29*

Chapter Four

42K Prop Wash, July 1942,
Sequoia Field.............................Author's Collection.......................*facing page 35*
Cadet 243, 42-K.......................Author's Collection.......................*facing page 41*

Chapter Five

Squadron I at Merced...........Author's Collection......................*facing page 45*
Ozzie at Carlsbad
with His 1936 Buick..............Author's Collection........................*facing page 51*

Chapter Seven

Ozzie Later at the
Controls of a B-29.................Author's Collection.......................*facing page 69*
Ozzie's Sketch of F.D.R.........Author's Collection.......................*facing page 73*
Bangor High Drama Club Performing
Prelude to Courage..........................1945 *Oracle*............................*facing page 79*

Chapter Eight

Script of Unfinished Play......Author's Collection.......................*facing page 85*
Austin's Army Air Force
Photograph............................Author's Collection.......................*facing page 89*

Chapter Nine
The Results of the
Mid-Air Collision.............497th Yearbook The Long Haul............*facing page 99*

Epilogue
Last Time Home,
Summer 1944..........................Author's Collection.....................*facing page 117*

Nancy Marcoux

Acknowledgements

On no other stage are the scenes shifted with a swiftness so like magic as on the great stage of history when once the hour strikes.

Ralph Bellamy's aphorism seems so appropriate to the topic of this book as it is the story of a young theater loving Maine man caught up on the stage of history and the unrelenting events of World War II. His story, while personal, methodically unfolds scene by scene.

I am indebted to those along the way who helped me tell Austin Rodney Keith's story. The help of Nancy J. Marcoux of Guilford, New Hampshire was invaluable. Years ago, Nancy and her husband Tom had taken in Austin's ailing sister Marion. The Marcouxs had come to know Marion as she was their daughter Alix's piano teacher. Marion, after a stay in the hospital and on a doctor's order that she could no longer live alone, asked Nancy and Tom if she could come and live with them. They said "Yes!" and took her in. With Marion, came all her things including many photos of Austin, a crucial letter, his military yearbooks, some of his writing, many supporting official letters, and many other primary documents. Miraculously, Tom and Nancy held on to these things even moving them to their new home overlooking Lake Winnepesaukee long after Marion had entered a nursing home and after her death in 2006. Nancy cheerfully dug these boxed materials out and eagerly shared them with me. Austin's story could not have been told with such depth and feeling without Nancy's help.

I am also appreciative of the help of the staff of the Special Collections Department of the Raymond H. Fogler Library, The University of Maine. Everyone cheerfully made every requested box of the Bricker Collection available, transporting them from storage to the third floor of the university's library. There, they used the opportunity to catalog the long stored materials. Heartfelt thanks to Elaine Smith, library assistant, Brenda Howitson Steeves, archivist/special collections librarian, and Josh Klimas, student library aide. It was Josh who found Austin's play at last in the 93rd box of the 95 box collection--a play that had not been seen for 65 years. Thanks goes to Deborah B. Averill, librarian of Bangor High School, friend and colleague. Debe spent many hot summer days helping me go through the files of the Bricker Collection. Also thanks to William Cook and Elizabeth A. Stevens of the Bangor Public Library for their assistance and to Dana Lippitt, curator of the Bangor Museum and Center for History for her help.

I am extremely grateful to Kathryn J. Olmstead, editor of *Echoes Magazine*. Kathryn graciously and promptly read each chapter and offered expert editorial suggestions to make the manuscript more readable. Finally, my appreciation goes to Laureen, my wife, for her support and understanding throughout this process of book writing.

Prologue

As a child growing up in the late 1940s, I remember hearing vague stories about the early years of that decade. My father was a ministerial student during the World War II years so he was exempt from military service. Uncles, though, served in the U. S. Navy or Army; one trained as a fighter pilot. They all came home. They quickly picked-up where they left off when the war for America broke out and seldom spoke about their wartime experiences. They lived their lives and had their chances; all are gone now.

The United States mobilized over 16 million men and women to fight Nazi Germany and Imperial Japan. Nearly one-half million men and women did not return. In the immediate years afterwards, towns and cities moved to memorialize its lost. In Bangor, Maine, the public library created a memorial book to honor the city's war dead. Along with a picture, a brief bibliographic entry prepared by family still notes the sacrifice of each.

Austin Rodney Keith is one of those young people in that memorial book. A handsome young man, a flier proudly displaying his wings on his uniform, his broad and contagious smile invites the thoughtful onlooker to want to know more about him. What were his dreams and ambitions? What dare he hope for his future? The brief narrative offers more clues. He was ambitious and talented--a writer and an actor. How far could he have gone? And then came the war.

This is Austin's story. Born in the tidal river city made famous by lumber, Bangor was Austin's home, and it nurtured him. Here, he found opportunity to dream, to write, and to act. He carried this bent with him when he enrolled in the fall of 1940 at the nearby University of Maine. There, he excelled in theater and made a name for himself. His last performance was ten days after Pearl Harbor.

Like so many of that time, Austin left for war service. This great venture took him to places far from his home--areas he had never heard of before. Austin trained as an air warrior but never let go of his dream for a future in theater. Wartime letters to his theater professor and mentor detail his passion. As months of war became years, though, Austin became keenly aware of his own mortality and knew like all citizens turned soldiers that he may not return home.

Austin had a job to do for his country, and he wanted to do it well. But he needed courage to overcome fear. For him, he worked out his conflict by using a theatrical convention to affirm his philosophy--his faith and perhaps that of others. He wrote a one act play titled *Prelude to Courage*. His play won a prize and gained him notoriety.

Austin and his crew landed in Saipan in early January, 1945. He was a pilot of the nation's most sophisticated mass weapon yet developed, the B-29 Superfortress. Soon, he and his men would join other crews as they made harrowing journeys across hundreds of miles of open ocean to bomb Japan. Death lingered nearby with every dangerous mission. In a remarkable late January letter to his parents, Austin foresaw his own demise, admitted his fear, but reassured his folks with his faith. His faith gave him the courage and strength to bravely lead his men into each combat mission.

Chapter One

Tokyo Bound

"What! is there a catch in this somewhere?"

Wayne Trenton,III in *Skidding*
played by Austin Rodney Keith
Bangor High School, May 21, 1937

Ponderous Peg languidly lifted off the end of the run-way and banked to the left out over the Pacific Ocean. She was one of hundreds of B-29 bombers leaving at one minute intervals and heading for Japan. At her controls, sat 1st Lieutenant Austin Rodney Keith, Airplane Commander. Lieutenant Wassil Katchmir sat in the co-pilot's seat to the right and across the expansive flight deck. Lt. Katchmir was a replacement for 2nd Lt. James B. Bunga. Heaquarters pulled Lt. Bunga from the crew just prior to this mission. Nine other crew members within the mammoth aircraft settled down and assumed their in-flight duties.

The day, Sunday, February 25, 1945, promised to be long and tedious. The men had already been up for three hours, and it was only 7:30 am. Japan was more than 1,400 hundred miles away--fourteen hundred miles over open ocean before the bombing mission on Tokyo could begin. If all went well, Ponderous Peg would touch down back on Saipan by late evening.

Lieutenant Keith brought the B-29 up to an altitude of 1500 feet. He would fly her there at that height until the wing assembly point where aircraft would go into formation, west of the Bonin Islands nearly three hours away. Flying at this altitude was easier on the airplane, for its load would be reduced somewhat by burning hundreds of gallons of gasoline before climbing to 25,000 feet for the bomb run. Ponderous Peg carried 5,000 pounds of bombs, all E46 incendiaries with just one 500-pound general purpose bomb used for spotting purposes to help photographers later assess the bomb damage.

Austin checked with his crew. Everyone was in good spirits. With the exception of Lt. Katchmir, the crew had trained together since the previous September. This was the fourth mission for the crew after arriving at Saipan on January 14. At first, things were very slow for the newcomers; Lt. Keith had complained to one of his college professors that: "I still haven't been on a raid, and the monotony of sitting around here is just beginning to get on my nerves." A change in command, though, of the XXI Bomber Command promised that the tempo of bombing would pick up. General Curtis LeMay replaced General Haywood Hansell Jr. in mid-January. LeMay knew that "...the new B-29s over there in the Marianas didn't seem to have been earning any Merit Badges. At least their performance wasn't satisfying Hap Arnold...," Commanding General of the U. S. Army Air Forces. Over 200 B-29s or Super Fortresses (Superforts) would take part in today's bombing mission but with a difference. Instead of precision bombing selected targets with conventional bombs as advocated by Hansell, bombers on this mission would release highly flammable incendiary bombs over Tokyo neighborhoods. American war planners believed that the Japanese had dispersed their war industries among residential neighborhoods. The bombers would still release their payloads from an altitude of 25,000 feet, but the new tactics promised better bombing results. In the island hopping campaign of the Pacific area, Japan had shown itself to be a formidable foe with a will to die over surrender. Pressure

Ponderous Peg Being Readied for a Mission

from Washington to bring Japan to her knees and soon was mounting.

Lt. Keith thought back to February 15. The crew had an earlier practice mission on Truk but this date was their first real combat mission. Bombers were scheduled to bomb Tokyo but were turned back by a severe cold front that broke up the tightly organized formations. He and others from his squadron bombed Hamamatsu instead. The weather played havoc with their second combat mission on the 19th of February, this time to Musashino. Lt. Keith, like other B-29 airplane commanders, was forced to drop his bombs through the cloud cover by using radar. The Army Air Forces had already learned that the weather over Japan was awful and was subject to dramatic change within short periods of time. This terrible weather was preventing precision bombing from having the desired effects. Austin knew the tactical importance of today's mission to the 73rd Wing and hoped that this time he and his 497th Bombardment Group would make it to over their Tokyo target without having to change plans prior to their bombing run.

Off Saipan, the weather was perfectly clear as Ponderous Peg roared northwestward at over 200 miles per hour. Austin thought the B-29 was "...tops..."; much of the war against Japan now depended on the massive bomber with a wing span nearly the width of a football field. Indeed, the B-29 represented the biggest wartime investment of the United States government at over $3.75 billion, outspending the Manhattan Project to develop an atomic bomb by more than a billion dollars. And ambitious men within the Army Air Forces hoped to show how bombing could swing the outcome of the war with Japan in favor of the United States. Perhaps then, Congress would separate the air arm from the

Army and let it stand alone as its own military branch.

Lt. Keith called his flight engineer on the ship's inter-phone for the latest performance information. The flight engineer, who sat immediately behind the co-pilot, faced an array of dials and instruments that measured the performance of the four Wright R-3300 18 cylinder radial engines. His job was to efficiently use every drop of fuel so that the aircraft would make it back to base after 15 hours of flying. The flight engineer also was responsible for monitoring the bomber's complex electrical and mechanical systems. Technical Sergeant Lawrence D. Helmke answered and said: "All instruments in the green." This expression meant that everything was functioning normally. Austin admired Larry, an unassuming 25-year-old from Woodburn, Indiana, for his thorough technical expertise. Helmke had enlisted in the Air Corps of the Army in 1940 long before the outbreak of hostilities. A graduate of Woodburn High School, he was married, and had an 18-month-old daughter named Rita Ann.

The navigator, 2nd Lt. Milton E. Smith Jr., called Lt. Keith to give him the latest crucial course headings. Milton sat behind the pilot and was one of the six crew men out of the ship's 11 who was housed within the greenhouse or front part of the bomber. Like Austin, Milton also had his wings but in the B-29 he was responsible for guiding the plane to its target. The crew would rely on him to guide them to the wing's assembly point, to provide the proper bearings to the target and arrive there on time, and to bring them home again over the expansive Pacific. He fit his role well for he was a serious young man, only 22, who had just married the summer before. But Austin could get "Milt" to smile, and when he did his eyes sparkled. Milton was born in St. Louis, Missouri, but

The Crew at Clovis Army Air Field, Fall 1944
First Row, Kneeling, Left to Right: Dugan, Seel, Flick, Coster, Caruso
Second Row, Standing, Left to Right: Bunga, Keith, Smith, Broitzman, Helmke

had grown up in Danville, Illinois. A talented artist, he was attending a commercial arts school in Indianapolis when he was inducted in 1942; he was an only child.

Diagonally across from Milton's work table sat Sgt. William M. Seel, the radio operator. Known as Mickey, Sgt. Seel was from Canaanville, Ohio, and graduated from Rome-Canaan High School in 1938. He entered the Army Air Forces in 1942. Mickey was a accomplished clarinetist who, while in high school, risked his life to rescue his clarinet from his parents' burning home. He always wore a smile and was well liked by the crew. He turned 25 the previous October. His older brother Peter flew for the Army's Air Transport Command. Mickey busied himself adjusting the VHF command radio used by Austin and the Collins HF 'Mixmaster' voice unit used for longer range communications. He also knew Morse Code, so essential to military operations.

The rising sun glared off the right panes of the aircraft's forward cockpit. Lt. Keith had never flown a plane with so much glass. While he thought the visibility was much improved over the B-17, he dreaded landing the aircraft as each pane of glass gave a distorted view of the runway especially at night when lights reflected off the glass at different angles. Today, all he hoped for was that when they returned to Isley Field tonight it wasn't raining as that made landing even more strenuous especially after 15 hours of flying. Austin decided to save that worry for later; he had enough to concern himself with now.

Austin continued to check in with his crew. Immediately to his front and slightly downward sat his bombardier, Flight Officer Robert C. Broitzman, 22, from Elgin, Illinois. In the B-29, the bombardier sat in the very front of the aircraft, surrounded by glass for a commanding view--a view that would help to assure bombing success. Like so many young men, Broitzman had left college to join the military and to do his part in the war effort. He was a senior at Illinois State Normal School majoring in music and theater when he enlisted in the spring of 1943. Austin, in a September 3 letter to Herschel Bricker, his theater professor at Maine, said: "He's studied concert piano for several years and gave his first formal recital a little over a year ago." But now he had his wings earned the previous July just before joining the crew in September. Austin thought a lot of Robert because they had similar interests in the arts. Austin, too, had left his college studies to go off and fight. And, like Broitzman, Austin hoped to return to college to complete his studies in theater after the war. Broitzman also resembled a friend Austin knew at the University of Maine, a coincidence which made him seem even closer. But Maine was distant now.

The six crewmen within the cockpit enjoyed the freedom that improvement in aircraft design brought over the course of the war. The pressurized control cabin meant that they did not have to wear the heated and bulky flying suits required of their fellow airmen flying the unpressurized B-17 and B-24 bombers. And above 10,000 feet, they did not have to don facial masks and go on bottled oxygen. Four other crewmen occupied another but separate pressurized area in the middle of the aircraft and beyond the bomb bays. A 35-foot-long tunnel connected this compartment with the crew in the cockpit area. Here, three gunners and a radar operator were located. These men would defend Ponderous Peg should she come under Japanese fighter attack. Key to their defense was the central fire control (CFC) system, an early computerized system operated by the CFC gunner, Sgt. Eugene A. Barry. Lt. Keith phoned Sgt. Barry. At 19, Sgt. Barry was the youngest

The B-29 Cockpit

man on the crew. He joined the others later in the fall of 1944 at Clovis Army Air Field after completing his specialized training. Tall and athletic, Barry played basketball and ran track at George Washington High School in Alexandria, Virginia where he graduated in 1943. Soon thereafter, he enlisted in the AAF.

Austin gave Barry and the other gunners permission to test fire the B-29's main armament of 50 caliber machine guns under their control. Left blister gunner, Sgt. Robert C. Flick fired from his pedestal sight to test his machine gun. Sgt. Flick, 22, was just made a sergeant on February 1. From Butler, Pennsylvania, he and his young wife were the proud parents of an infant son, Richard Leo. Opposite Flick on the right blister was Sgt. Charles R. Dugan of Amsterdam, New York, a small industrial city on the Erie Canal. He had just turned 20 on December 7. For Charles, his birth date had more than the usual meaning especially now. He grew up with his aunts and graduated high school from St. Mary's Institute in 1943.

Austin then called the fourth man in this section of the aircraft who worked within a windowless compartment operating the AN/APQ-13 radar. Sgt. Lloyd H. Coster responded to the airplane commander's questions about the radar equipment with reassuring confidence; everything was operational. Radar was a new innovation within the B-29 bomber and essential to bombing success. And today, probably because of Japan's frequent cloud cover, they might need to use the radar which could detect ground targets forward of the aircraft. Sgt. Coster worked closely with the bombardier. From Rochester, New York, Coster went by his middle name Howard, but the crew called him Howie. He was a student at Bradley College in Peoria, Illinois, when he enlisted in January 1943. Only 21, he was newly married during the fall of 1944. Austin attended his wedding.

At the very rear of the aircraft sat the tail gunner. He occupied a third but cramped pressurized area only accessible through a door off the mid-section. Lt. Keith called Sgt. Luigi Caruso, 27, through the airplane's inter-phone and gave him permission to test fire the 50 caliber machine guns under his control and the 20 mm cannon that protruded from the tail. Austin thought of him as "...a jolly little Italian fellow...." From Woodbridge, Connecticut, Caruso was inducted, like Austin, at Fort Devens, Massachusetts, in 1942. He was the shortest member of the crew. The crew relied on him to ward off any Japanese fighter attacks from the rear.

2nd Lt. Wassil Katchmir was new to the crew. But he was a good replacement for Lt. Bunga. Lt. Katchmir came from the 468th Bombardment Group and had been in the Army Air Forces since before the war began. One of nine children, he was from Jonestown, Pennsylvania, and was married. He had just turned 28 years old in January and was the oldest member of the crew.

For Austin, being in charge of so large a crew was a new and challenging experience but one he readily accepted. "To these boys I am brother, mother, boss, and father-confessor. It should really be a wonderful experience for me (and I hope for them)," he wrote in a letter to Bricker. Austin thought of his crew as a "...pretty swell bunch of boys...." Within a few hours, though, the crew of Ponderous Peg would be in combat and all their training individually and as a fighting unit would be severely tested.

The Crew at Saipan, January 1945
First Row, Kneeling, Left to Right: Bunga, Broitzman, Smith, Keith
Second Row, Standing, Left to Right: Seel, Flick, Barry,
Caruso, Dugan, Coster, Helmke

As Ponderous Peg continued to drone northwestward, Austin looked down at the vast, shimmering Pacific and wondered what the day would bring. All were safe for now within the cocoon of the giant bomber. But to Austin, the 1500 feet between the aircraft and the water's surface represented the distance between life and uncertainty.

Ponderous Peg was not the aircraft that the crew had flown in from Kearney, Nebraska, to Saipan, a trip of more than 10 days. Their aircraft was a B-29 they named The Ghastly Goose. Austin now thought of the fate of that aircraft that he and his crew had come to love. Following an Army Air Forces tradition, Austin's crew named their new glistening silver craft while still training in Nebraska. Most crews, though, chose female names that provoked sexually explicit or hidden meanings. But many on Austin's crew were already married. Out of good taste, then, they chose to make fun of the bomber's appearance. Once in the combat zone, though, it was not unusual for the crew to be separated from its aircraft depending upon the bombardment group's need for ready aircraft and the crew's readiness for combat. On January 27, Captain Dale Peterson and crew flew The Ghastly Goose on a mission to Hamamatsu as part of the 497th Bombardment Group's bombing mission. This particular day, the bombers came under pounding attack from Japanese fighters over Mount Fuji and The Ghastly Goose was badly damaged when it was rammed in a wing by a Japanese fighter. This was a new and deadly technique used by desperate Japanese pilots. With excessive fuel loss from the ramming, Peterson successfully ditched the bomber in the water off the coast of Japan. Another B-29 radioed the downed aircraft's position to rescue operations while crew members scurried onto the wings of the bomber. But, a storm broke out and the entire crew was lost.

Austin and his crew felt they were lucky in having Ponderous Peg to fly. This bomber had a storied reputation within the 497th as a tough ship that came through despite odds against it. Nearly a month before Austin and crew arrived in Saipan, Ponderous Peg was damaged in battle over Japan with both engines on the right side disabled. Miraculously, Ponderous Peg flew the nearly 1500 miles back over open ocean and safely landed at Isley with no injuries to crew. Lt Keith hoped that today Ponderous Peg's luck would hold and that she would bring his crew back safely.

Lt. Keith needed a break so he turned over flying the giant aircraft to his co-pilot, 2nd Lt. Katchmir. Wassil eagerly took over. Austin then stretched out, peered out over the open ocean, and began to ponder how he happened to be here in this time and in this place. Words from his past "...What! is there a catch in this somewhere?..." suddenly came to him. He thought of his past growing up in Bangor, Maine, his hometown on the Penobscot River.

The Ghastly Goose Nose Art by Lt. Milt Smith, Navigator

Chapter Two

He Loved to Play a Part

> "You bad? Consound it, Tom Sawyer, your're just old pie ' longside of what I am. Oh, lordy, lordy, lordy, I wisht I only had half your chance."
>
> Huckleberry Finn, in *The Adventures of Tom Sawyer*
> played by Austin Rodney Keith
> Bangor High School, December 11, 1936

Magnificent and majestic elms arched over virtually every street and lane that spread out from Bangor's commercial center. Nineteenth century mansions and modest homes characterized neighborhoods across its hilly terrain, and church steeples pierced the sky. For Edgar and Bertha Keith, Bangor was the perfect place to settle down, have a business, and raise a family. The tidal city along the shores of the Kenduskeag and Penobscot rivers had developed into a commercial and service center for all of eastern Maine. Although Bangor was no longer the "1870s lumber capital of the world" by the 1920s, it remained prosperous.

Edgar met Bertha in Aroostook County. He was newly discharged from the U.S. Army after WWI service. Bertha, born in Perham, had known hardship early on. Her mother died while she and her older sister Pearl were still teenagers. Her father, Forrest Tibbetts, carried on as best he could with his hardware store in New Sweden, the thriving farming village of Swedish immigrants founded in 1870. Bertha was close to her sister and to her father even after he remarried. Edgar and Bertha were married in Caribou June 19, 1918. Shortly thereafter, they moved to Bangor.

At first, the Keiths lived on Tyler Avenue, a curved street that bordered Mt. Pleasant Cemetery on the very edge of the developed city. Further west on Ohio Street, dairy farms occupied the open countryside to the edge of the city's limits. Here in this house that still stands in a neighborhood little changed, the Keith's first child, a boy, was born on Sunday, April 13, 1919. Four days later, with both grandfathers present, his parents named him Austin Rodney Keith. His grandfather Tibbetts gave him a baby carriage while his grandfather Keith gave him a ring. Family members speculated on what Austin might become: his grandfather Keith hoped he would be a minister, preferably Baptist, while Aunt Fern, Edgar's sister, speculated that he would become a musician and singer. His father thought a lawyer sounded good; his mother hoped he would be a professional of some sort. No one proffered a B-29 pilot.

The Keith family lived on lower Cedar Street near Davenport Park later on. Austin started elementary school at the Valentine School just around the corner. Edgar and Bertha bought a house at 10 Boynton Street, near Court Street in March 1928. This home was closer to the city's center where Edgar worked and later where he had an appliance store and a bowling alley. Austin finished elementary school at the Bower Street School at the corner of Ohio and Court streets. Near his home on his way to and from school, he passed Coe Park, one of many of Bangor's inviting neighborhood parks, where Austin would stop and play with friends. He was lively and energetic, curious and friendly.

When Austin was nearly eight years old, his sister Marion Louise was born on January 30, 1927. Austin and his sister formed a close bond despite the wide age gap between them. And later in life, like her brother, Marion developed an in-

10 Boynton Street

terest in the arts, especially in music.

Austin participated in many boyhood sports and activities. Often, much to the consternation of his mother, he boxed in the house with his father, a champion bowler and golfer. But it was only for fun.

At twelve, Austin had a paper route on the east side of the city, and, in a contest typical of the early 1930s, he sold enough papers to win a trip to Washington, D. C. as part of the Newspaper Boys Pilgrimage. When asked about it he said: "It is all just like a dream...At first I didn't think that I had a chance to win the contest. And I was embarrassed when I first started calling on people that I didn't know, and explained how they could have the paper delivered to them every day of the week for six months. And when I told them that all they would have to pay was 15 cents a week, why the rest was simple. It seemed that almost everyone I saw wanted the paper....Believe me I am glad that I am going to Washington...Just think, I've never seen a president--that is, outside the movies." He and the other newspaper boys toured historic sites and met President Hoover.

For junior high school, Austin went to the Hannibal Hamlin School at Union Place, where Union and Hammond streets cross. There, he began to show a predilection for the dramatic arts. As a seventh grader, he acted in skits and programs for school assemblies and sought dramatic involvement of some sort even if it were in making the scenery. He concerned his teachers at times with his "dreaming," perhaps because he didn't appear to be paying much attention to his studies. He wrote parodies of songs, and he loved to imitate popular personalities such as Chevalier, Barrymore, Gable, and Crosby. And Austin was a good dancer particularly in The Swing.

In recognition of that talent, he took on the nickname Ozzie after the popular 1930s radio dance band leader Ozzie Nelson. This moniker would stay with him throughout high school, into college, and beyond.

September 6, 1933, Austin entered Bangor High School on Harlow Street. The substantial classical building was built in 1913 after the great Bangor fire of 1911 destroyed the old high school which stood across the street. The new high school had a beautiful auditorium with a spacious stage that lent itself to dramatic productions. Here for the first time, the public would see Austin's dramatic talent.

Austin's academic performance in the classical curriculum was mixed throughout high school with one notable exception, military drill. The Army Reserve Officer Training Corps, still available to Bangor High School students today, gave Austin the opportunity to excel. He was a member of the Officers' Club by the fall of 1936 and rose to the rank of captain.

Austin was known to his fellow students as a genuine, kind young man. He was handsome with light brown hair and blue eyes and stood at five feet ten inches tall. The girls took notice. For a while, he went out with Elizabeth "Bette" Barker who remembered him as "...pleasant, thoughtful, generous, good looking, affable, gentlemanly, fun to be with. He was just a generally nice guy."

During high school, despite his average academic performance in the traditional subject matter, he began to show extraordinary abilities in creative writing and dramatic performance. In those days, Bangor High School students published a literary magazine six times a year called *Oracle*.

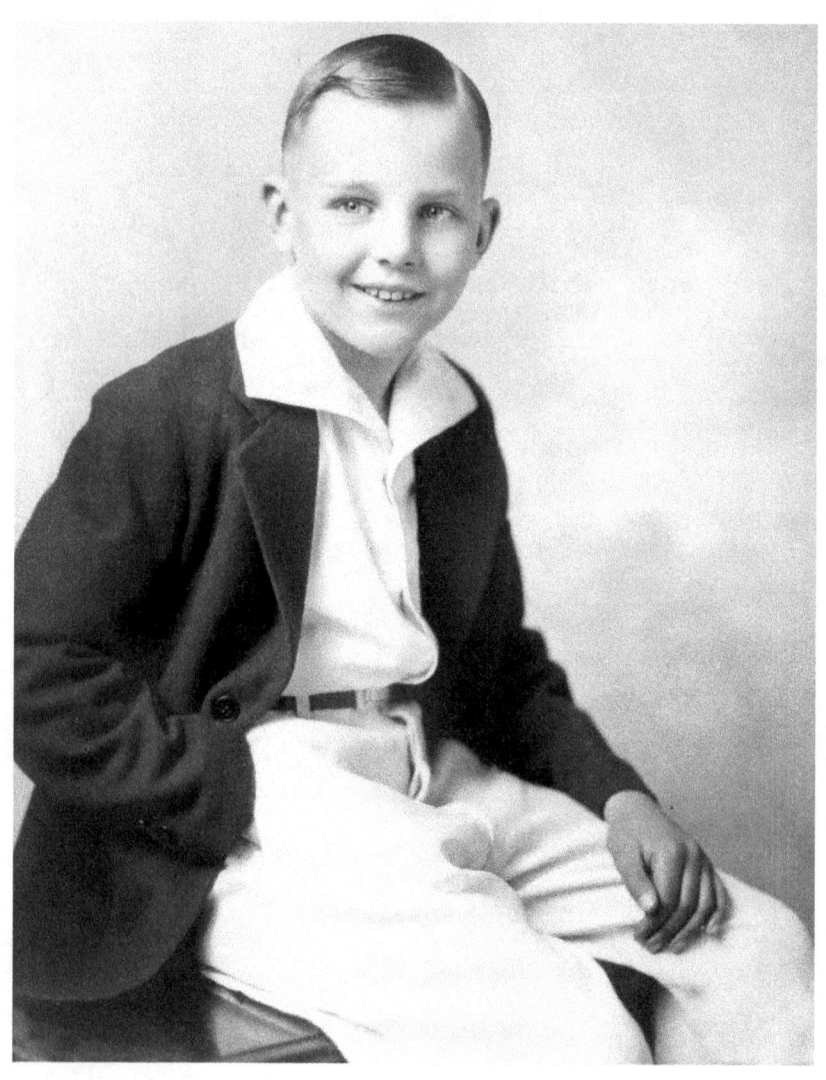

Austin at 10

He Loved to Play a Part 15

The June edition served as the school's yearbook. Austin's first story appeared in the February 1936 edition. He was a junior. Titled "A Slight Mistake," this story weaves a tale of a bank teller, Milt Blake, gone bad. Milt's uncle, the local newspaper publisher, bails him out financially several times until he refuses to do so any further. Now, Milt has new debts for gambling and the bookie threatens to tell his bank. So, on the sly, Milt takes the gambling debt from the bank's vault hoping not to be discovered. But he must return the money within a few days. Meanwhile, a notorious bank robber escapes. Milt reads about this in a torn copy of his uncle's newspaper that has text missing. Part of the robber's description reads that the robber "...lks with slight lisp." Letters are missing because of the torn copy. This text is enough, though, for Milt to hatch a clandestine plan. Late that night, Milt attacks the watchman while speaking with a lisp, thereby, in his mind and as he read the story, pretending to be the escaped robber. He enters the bank and steals $10,000. In setting the type for the story about the escaped bank robber, however, Milt's uncle had misspelled a word. Instead of "lisp", he meant "limp". Also, the first two letters of the word in the torn newspaper were "wa" not "ta" as Milt assumed. A corrected copy read "...walks with a limp." This sudden turn of events, based on word misuse and human assumption, implicates Milt as committing the crime.

Austin's second story, "I'll Take Basketball," appeared in December 1936. In this narrative, Austin tells the story of a much overworked athlete who is number one for his school in football, basketball, baseball, and track. Tired of the pressure to perform and to be "a champion," he goes on a deer hunting trip deep into the Maine woods with his father. This trip promises to be relaxing and carefree. Late in the day, the athlete sees a buck and fires at him. Unfortunately, he also wounds a large unseen black bear who comes charging at him and swipes him in the shoulder. The father kills the angry bear in the nick of time and saves his son from mortal injury. Reflecting on the day's events, the athlete decides that sports are not so bad after all, hence the title of the story. Austin also illustrated his stories.

"The Future Lies Ahead" is a fanciful story by Austin that predicts space travel to Mars. It appeared in the March 1937 edition of the *Oracle* and used imaginative terms to describe flight within the solar system. Austin also foresaw some of the equipment needed for space travel taken for granted today. Austin predicted launch pads and computer screens that he calls "visiplates". Propulsion of the rocket ship into space is by a large rocket, today called a booster rocket, that was used for taking off and once in space, the rocket stopped firing. Austin moves the rocket ship by means of smaller propulsion rockets, as found on today's spacecraft. He writes "...and the others were firing smoothly and almost noiselessly." He calculates speed with a term he calls "...dynoes..." to represent faster travel than miles per hour and long before the term "Mach speed" came into usage. To ward off any attempted pirating of the space ship and crew by bandits, Austin gives crew members a "...paralysis gun...", now called a taser gun, to use. Austin calls the large passenger rocket ship, or shuttle, a "...hexogolets...", named after its inventor, Professor Hexogolet. Austin includes items in an exhibit at the "...Natural Museum on Earth..." such as "...a 1937 Cadillac, a Boeing pursuit plane, and many other oddities..." that reflected his own time. His classmates acknowledged his futuristic imagination on the flyleaf of the *Oracle*: " Austin, like the soothsayers, seems to be able to see into the far-distant future...." He was just 17.

"An enormous black bear came charging across the clearing."

**Illustration from "I'll Take Basketball"
Drawn by Austin**

Austin made his acting debut to a Bangor audience on Friday evening, December 11, 1936, in the play, *The Adventures of Tom Sawyer* adapted for stage by Charles George. Austin played the part of the mischievous Huckleberry Finn. This story was a favorite of the audiences of the 1930s; the cast really had to perform to meet expectations. A review that appeared in the Bangor Daily News the next day summarized Austin's performance:

> Austin Keith as Huckleberry Finn was vivacious, skillful, sure. In spite of the playwright, one Charles George, Keith managed what at times seemed a virtual impossibility--bringing out the real Huckleberry Finn of Mark Twain's conception. Not the actor's fault, surely, was it that the author had seen fit to moralize, yea, even sanctify, the irresponsible young ragamuffin so dear to the hearts of American readers. Double praise, then to youth Keith, who had his own, and true, ideas of the role, and who succeeded in rising above the triteness and Sunday-school atmosphere of many of the lines that were put into his mouth

In the spring of his senior year, Austin was involved in another play put on by the Dramatic Club. This production was titled *Skidding*, a clever comedy by Aurania Rouverol that considered the havoc brought to family dynamics by women's equality. It became known to American moviegoers in the late 1930s as *A Family Affair* with Mickey Rooney and Lionel Barrymore. Austin played the part of Wayne Trenton, III, a young suitor from a well-to-do New York family who was after an Idaho judge's daughter. Austin played his part with "...excellent effect..." according to a Bangor Daily News review published on Saturday, May 22, 1937, the day after the performance.

Despite his theatrical triumphs and literary accomplishments during his senior year, Austin did not achieve his goal of winning an appointment to West Point Military Academy. As cadet captain of Company A, Bangor High School R.O.T.C., though, Austin won a medal for the best drill performance of a company at the 1937 review and inspection held at Broadway Park. Though not an outstanding player in any one sport, Austin liked sports and cheered on the teams from the sidelines. In academics, he earned only average grades, with the exception of A's in Military Drill. Indeed, for the second quarter of his senior year, his teachers gave him a poor grade for conduct, which in those days meant effort. He was too busy living out his theatrical dreams.

Undaunted by his failure to be accepted to West Point, Austin enrolled for a post-graduate year. He repeated several core academic subjects, but showed limited improvement. He remained enrolled in Military Drill in which he continued to earn straight A's. During this post-graduate year, 1937-1938, Austin went out with Bette Barker. She was a senior in the college preparatory program, and he continued to be active in the life of Bangor High School. During this period, Austin wrote another imaginative story for the *Oracle*. Titled "Army Fights," this story is about a championship boxing match between West Point Military Academy and Annapolis Naval Academy. He was familiar with boxing terms learned from his dad which he wove into the story. The story is full of action and surprise, hallmarks of Austin's tales. The end result is that West Point wins the contest. The cadets celebrate their victory on the train all the way back to campus. Perhaps, in some bittersweet way, Austin wished he were part of the cadet revelers.

A highlight of Austin's postgraduate year was the annual

The Officer's Club on the Front Steps of Bangor High School
Austin, Fourth from Left, Front Row

R.O.T.C. military ball held in May of 1938. He was captain of the cadets, and Bette was the "honorary cadet captain." It was a gala affair held in the school's ornate auditorium. Austin was "striking" in his military uniform; Bette received a miniature scabbard and blade as a souvenir.

Bette graduated in June and would start at the University of Maine in the fall. That summer, she and Austin, along with his family, climbed Mount Katahdin. This outing in this beautiful but rugged part of the state included camping at Chimney Pond and crossing the famous "Knife Edge." It was a trip to remember. By the fall of 1938, no appointment to West Point was in the offing for Austin. Bette and Austin continued to see each other occasionally and remained friends, but Bette wanted to be able to meet new people at the university. Uncertain as to what to do next and discouraged, Austin worked in his father's bowling alley, The Bowlaway that was located on York Street near Exchange in downtown Bangor. His father had started this business in the mid-thirties after he founded the Electric Appliance Corporation, which was located a few blocks away. There, he sold a variety of appliances from a store at 35 Park Street. During high school, Austin had helped out there after school. Austin's aunt Pearl, his mother's sister who also lived with the family at 10 Boynton Street, was the bookkeeper and a director.

These few years must have been a difficult time for Austin as he pondered his future. Edgar Keith, Austin's father and now his boss, was somewhat demanding and domineering, and Austin was no longer involved in the spirited life of an educational institution. In personality, Austin was much more like his mother, Bertha, who was very gentle, good natured and kind.

During and after high school, Austin attended the Citizens Military Training Camp held each summer for a month at Fort McKinley in Portland. The last summer there, 1938, he served as adjutant to Major Robert Finnigan, commanding officer of the First Battalion. The CMTC camps across the nation were authorized by the National Defense Act of 1920 to voluntarily prepare young men as officers. Generally, they were not successful as few students, including Austin, attended for the four summers required to earn a commission as a second lieutenant. Attendance at the CMTC for Austin, though, provided a connection to and continuation of the military training he had enjoyed in high school. Austin still hoped for an appointment to West Point.

As Austin tried to sort out his life, he and his childhood friend Charles Bartlett hitchhiked one summer across the country. Charles, known as "Bubs", lived around the corner from Austin (Ozzie) on Ohio Street. He left Bangor High before his senior year to attend Deerfield Academy prior to going to LeHigh University. Over the years, Ozzie and Bubs were the closest of friends, almost like brothers; they were inseparable. During the summer of 1939, Bubs and Ozzie traveled to Washington D. C.

The winter snows of 1939-1940 in Bangor began to recede by mid-March. The world, it seemed, had started to unravel. War broke out in Europe the previous September. The Japanese in the Pacific continued to be restive in Southeast Asia while consolidating their gains in China. At home, Congress talked about a "peace-time" draft and calling up the National Guard. President Roosevelt, though, assured citizens that the United States would stay out of the war in Europe. In January 1940, Congressman Ralph O. Brewster of Maine's Third District designated Austin as "Second Alternate to

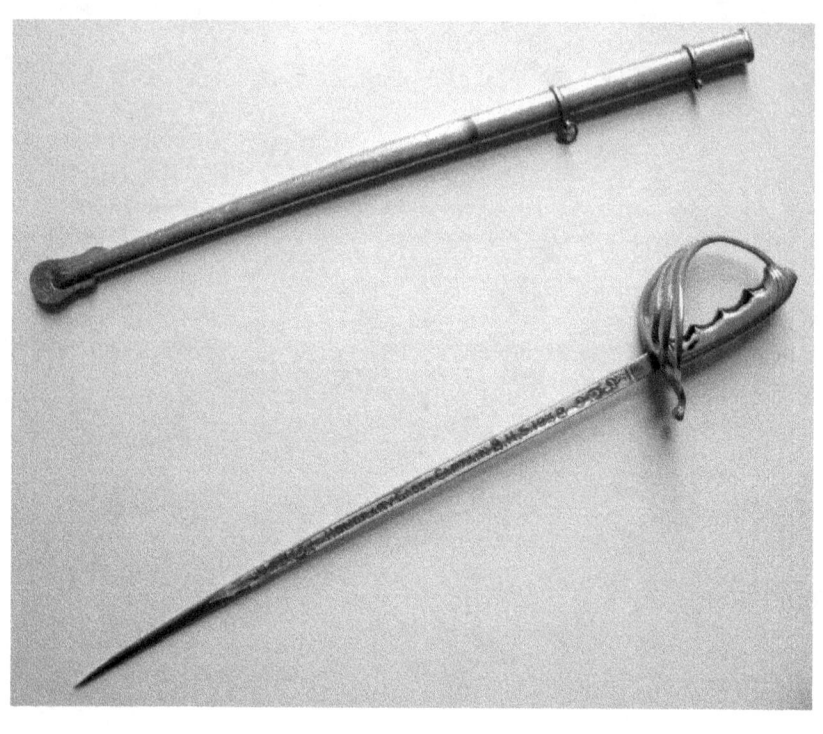

Souvenir Scabbard and Blade
Script Reads: Honorary Cadet Captain B.H.S 1938

West Point in accordance with the results of the recent Civil Service examination." Austin considered his chances for West Point as slim, though, as it depended upon the Principal Appointment and First Alternate failing. Meanwhile, Austin applied to enter the University of Maine for fall, 1940.

Chapter Three

Too Quickly Passed These Days

> "I can only remember a few nights as beautiful as this...."
>
> Nat Miller, in *Ah Wilderness!*
> played by Austin Rodney Keith
> Maine Masque Theatre, The University of Maine
> April 28-May 1, 1941

A fresh breeze blew across the Stillwater River up the gradual hill and through the Orono, Maine, campus on that sunny day in September 1940. More than 500 freshmen gathered in front of the columned granite Carnegie Library for the freshmen class photograph. Austin was there dressed in a sports jacket with tie. For him, it was a new beginning after graduating three years before from Bangor High School.

The University of Maine was a campus of 2,000 students. Most buildings sat on the edge of the hill that overlooked the river below. Vast open acreage spread to the east and to the north. The university had weathered the years of the Depression, but most buildings dated from the early part of 20th century or earlier. Yet, change was in the wind. Confident of the future, the trustees had instituted a plan to expand the pretty campus with badly needed academic buildings and laboratories around a new quad. Central to this plan was a new library, a magnificent colonial structure that symbolized the university's future importance. Arthur A. Hauck was president.

Students in the routine of college life gave little thought to world events that increasingly filled the daily newspapers.

Football Cheering Squad, 1940
Austin, Back Row, Second from Left

France fell to the Nazis in June and the Battle of Britain was underway. England seemed remote. Congress instituted a "peace time draft" and called up the National Guard for a year of service. But 1940 was a presidential election year and President Roosevelt hoped to keep the United States out of the European war. The death of the popular football star and graduate of the Class of 1937 James F. Dow in an Air Corps training accident in Queens, New York, that June, though, had grieved the campus and reminded people there that even Maine could be touched by war-related events happening elsewhere. But few freshmen knew of him, so for them, as for all freshmen classes, this was the start of the "best years of their lives."

Austin wasted no time in becoming involved in campus life. That fall, he joined the staff of the university's student newspaper, *The Maine Campus*, as a cub reporter. He wrote about the fall football season, traditionally popular with Maine students and community. And he was one of five male cheerleaders for the football squad that fall along with six coeds.

He also joined the Maine Masque, a student theatrical group, that drew the most participation of all student activities on campus barring athletics. Its director was faculty member Herschel L. Bricker. When still a young man, Bricker came to the university in the late 1920s as director of backstage activities for the Masque. By the mid-1930s, and after a year's fellowship with the Rockefeller Foundation, he returned to Maine as director of dramatics. Increasingly, he added more sophisticated theatrical courses and introduced challenging but popular plays, two each semester. By the fall of 1940, Bricker hoped to offer the uncut version of Shakespeare's *Hamlet*, no little undertaking for the small university.

Students were not automatically accepted into the Maine Masque without first being questioned by Bricker. Questions were reflective and searching as: "When did you first become interested in the theatre? Can you account for the germ that stimulated this interest? What estimate do you have of your own ability? Outline what you would like to do toward furthering your theater education, if given the opportunity? What do you believe to be necessary to your training as an actor?" and, "How do you develop characterization?" For aspiring thespians, though, Bricker's question, "Do you feel your part, or do you rely entirely upon acting technique?," was perhaps most poignant. Austin passed his questioning and was actively involved by early spring, 1941.

For two years, Bricker looked over his Masque students searching for the crucial role of Hamlet. He found his Hamlet in Earle Rankin, a sophomore student from Melrose, Massachusetts, who entered the university in 1939. Rankin went on to play key roles in Masque productions while at Maine. For Austin, involvement in theater once again gave expression to his creativity and imagination. He became a key participant and contributor to the Masque's success over the coming semesters. And, he made many close friends, Earle Rankin being his closest--a friendship that would stretch into time beyond his years at Maine.

Bricker scheduled *Hamlet* for March 1941. Austin tried out and was cast as Rosencrantz. He also served as an assistant stage manager. The rehearsal schedule was grueling, often stretching long into the evenings including Sunday.

Sharp late winter winds blew around the corners of Alumni Hall on Monday evening March 10th as students, faculty, and guests crowded into the "Little Theater" on the second floor.

Austin as Rosencrantz
From Left to Right: Austin, Earle Rankin as Hamlet,
William Brown as Guildenstern

Excitement and anticipation filled the air at 7p.m. when the lights dimly illuminated a midnight scene before Elsinore Castle, and Shakespeare's greatest tragedy began to unfold. Elsinore's ornate Room of State, with "...royal purple hangings, massive stone walls, and stained glass windows...was the most spectacular stage setting ever devised for a Masque play."

Hamlet ran late into the evening with two intermissions scheduled. But the performance was spectacular given its challenges for the small university. Earle Rankin performed masterfully throughout despite the exhausting demands of his role. Austin's performance as Rosencrantz along with that of William Brown as Guildenstern brought "...real polish to their appearances." The play ran every night that week except Friday with a special Saturday matinée for high school students. The Masque scheduled one last performance to benefit the "war relief program" on Thursday evening March 20. An ocean away, Rommel was chasing the British across North Africa.

Austin was thrilled. It was nearly four years since his last performance on stage as a senior at Bangor High School. And Professor Bricker liked his performance: "The two young men, Austin Keith and Bill Brown, playing Rosencrantz and Guildenstern respectively, were handsome, 'average Joe College,' who left the impression of being less familiar with court procedures, but who were brought there by Claudius, in hope that they, through their college friendships might snap Hamlet out of his better shack; men who could, like many college men, when together talk in double meaning."

Later that spring at the annual Masque banquet in May, Austin and Bill Brown had some fun with *Hamlet* when, as a spoof, they put on a skit titled "THE REINCARNATION OF HAMLET or 'The Play that Laid the Golden Egg and Became Omelet.'" Roseypants Keith and Guildenbottom Brown directed this farce. Bill played Herschel Bricker while Ozzie (Austin) played Hamlet. Bill and Ozzie convinced a number of other students to play key parts. "Your guess is as good as ours" played the part of The Ghost, though. The "tongue in cheek" comedy listed credits for hair styles as Keith and Brown, beauticians, costumes, Brown, Keith, and Co., artillery, Brown and Keith, hardware, and credits for the play itself as "Who the hell wants credit for it???" It was a performance of lively imagination and pure fun.

Earlier that spring, the Masque performed Eugene O'Neill's *Ah Wilderness!* as its second production for the semester. This play provided a nice contrast to the weighty *Hamlet*. Bricker said, "That the play contains real American patriotic spirit, is a reminder of the American way, and yet has plenty of laughs." Austin landed the part of the fatherly Nat Miller, a major role. For him, it was an acting victory; he was ebullient. *Ah Wilderness!* was a popular play of the day. George M. Cohan played Nat Miller on the New York stage on the east coast while Will Rogers played this part on the west coast. Lionel Barrymore played the part of Nat Miller in the movie version. Opposite Austin was Earle Rankin who played Richard, Nat Miller's sometimes questioning and philosophically errant son.

Ah Wilderness! ran from April 28 to May 1. Again the Little Theater was packed for each performance. Austin's performance was superb. "Mr. Keith enacts it agreeably, if not always authoritatively with an appreciation of the author's bright lines," wrote Oscar Shepard, theater critic for *The Bangor Daily News*. *The Maine Campus* commented on Ozzie's

Ozzie as Nat Miller

performance as: "Acting honors went to Austin Keith as the understanding father in a difficult situation. His portrayal was never forced and his mannerisms and reading of lines were always natural. He did not fail to get across the humor of the situation, but he did not force the comedy of any scene upon the audience." Austin thought: "...I can only remember a few nights as beautiful as this...."

The spring semester 1941 came to a close in late May with finals. Ozzie felt proud of his freshmen year. He adjusted well to college academically, he had made many friends, he became a brother in Beta Theta Pi fraternity, and he re-entered with public acclaim what he loved the most, theater. Austin began to dream of a career on the stage. He could hardly wait for the fall 1941 semester to start!

Ozzie started his sophomore year at the university in mid-September. The warm sunlit days and cool nights were invigorating and refreshing. Yet, on the horizon, dark forbidding clouds of man's making threatened interruption, distraction, and perhaps, destruction. The war in Europe had deteriorated with Nazi Germany's sweep into the Soviet Union, and England needed material help to continue to hold on. Lend Lease was underway. FDR and Churchill had met just the month before and announced The Atlantic Charter. For the Japanese, the collapse of the French and Dutch governments in Europe promised easy conquest of their colonial possessions in Southeast Asia which were rich in natural resources.

Austin didn't think too much about world events; he drilled every Saturday morning with R.O.T.C., something required of all male students. And he registered for Selective Service. Otherwise, his active life at the university continued. Ozzie wrote for the *The Maine Campus* weekly as a star reporter and was in charge of press releases.

By early October, Professor Bricker announced that the first play for the new year was the *The Golden Apple*. This was an original musical comedy by two senior students, Beatrice Besse and Frank Hanson. The year earlier, the talented pair won an ASCAP (The American Society of Composers, Authors and Publishers) award with their original production titled *Of Cabbages and Kings*. Their new production included 10 original musical scores and called for a cast of 58 students. Bricker scheduled performances to run from November 3 through November 6.

The comedy centers on Greek mythology with a modern twist. Jupiter's daughters constantly bicker over who deserves the "golden apple" for being the most beautiful. The exasperated god, banishes his daughters from Mount Olympus until they can resolve the matter among themselves. The action moves to the Waldorf-Astoria where the three sisters continue to argue among themselves until a newspaperman devises a plan to decide who is the most beautiful. Austin Keith played the role "of the harassed Jupiter. " The show was a resounding success.

That fall, Ozzie took an acting class, one of the new courses added to the theater program by Professor Bricker. This course culminated with a staged production by the acting class of the contemporary play by William Saroyan, *Jim Dandy-Fat Man in a Famine*. Somewhat avant-garde, the play has no plot. " It does not begin, it does not go anywhere, and it does not end." To Saroyan, critic Milton Ellis wrote, "...the play does not do or tell things, it is things....Life itself, at its most absurd and inconsequential, is more substantial, and

Austin as Johnny
Left to Right: Austin and Howell Runion as Little Johnny

not so pointless as this." This abstract play required consummate acting in order to deliver its theme effectively to the audience. Ozzie played Johnny and "...fitted admirably into the part..." with "...sufficient gravity." Earle Rankin played the part of Jock, and Bette Barker was Molly. *Jim Dandy* was performed 10 days after Pearl Harbor.

The United States was in turmoil from the "sudden and deliberate" Japanese attack. Three days later, Hitler declared war on the United States. Over the past few years, the U.S. government had begun to build up its forces primarily for a defensive role if needed. Even close to where Ozzie lived in Bangor, the U.S. Army built an airfield that was later called Dow Field. But now, since the attack on the U.S. Pacific fleet, the United States was looked to by the struggling democracies already at war to lead an offensive attack on two fronts against the Axis powers. College aged men were of prime military age and were seen by the government as providing badly needed military leadership.

In his unpublished autobiography, Herschel Bricker recalled this time for his students when early in 1942, "Austin Keith, Earl Rankin, Clark Kuney, Fred Libby, Dayson Decourcy, Bill Brown, Louis Chadwick, and Gerard Goulette--all among my finest and most active actors of the 1930-1940 decade--sat in my office and speculated about their immediate futures. They had been the backbone of the Maine Masque Theatre over the past one to four years....At this office bull session, these eight men were speculating on when they might be called to serve. Fred Libby, for example, expected to be called up almost immediately. It was my pleasure to inform Fred and the others that the government had already requested college men to remain <u>put</u> until they were summoned. A sigh of relief went around the circle, but each man knew, deep in his heart, that it was only of the instance--that all able-bodied men would be in battle before too many moons. Earle Rankin, the boy who had played Hamlet with deep e-motional feeling and eloquent sensitivity, was equally emotional and sensitive about war, about fighting, not so much for himself, but for his friends and theater teammates....The others all seemed better adjusted, probably because they were more inhibited or more skillful about hiding their emotions, to awaiting fate's answer to their question."

Austin, did not need wait long; he was drafted. He reported for duty at Fort Devens and was assigned to Coast Artillery January 26, 1942.

Chapter Four

Up, Up, and Away

> " Truly, and I hold
> ambition of so airy and light a quality
> that it is but a shadow's shadow."
>
> Rosencrantz, in *Hamlet*, Act II, Sc.II,
> Line 267-268
> played by Austin Rodney Keith
> The Maine MasqueTheatre, March 10-15, 1941
> The University ofMaine

Austin arrived at the Air Corps Replacement Training Center in Santa Ana, California mid-April 1942. Back east, first at Fort Devens then at Fort Eustis, Austin underwent testing and classification procedures and advocated for himself with the U.S. Army that he should be assigned to the Army Air Forces rather than to the infantry. He succeeded and became part of a quota that staff officers selected for air cadet training. The new cadets hoped to train at Maxwell Field in Alabama as it was closer to home, but instead the Army shipped them to sunny California. When the new air cadets arrived there, though, it wasn't so sunny--it rained and rained. To make matters worse, the installation, like so many across the country at that time, was so new that the barracks weren't ready. Austin and the other air cadets moved into tents.

Just after Austin arrived at Santa Ana, he received a 23rd birthday card from his folks back in Bangor, Maine. His father proudly addressed the card: " Cadet Austin Rodney Keith" and recalled their time together during a short leave home before he left for air cadet training, exhorting Austin to "develop mentally, physically, and morally." On the backside of the birthday card, his mother wrote: "Twenty-three years ago tomorrow pm, we were blessed with your arrival. Dad wanted to know how long that it would be before he could fly kites with you. And later you did fly kites together." Their boy would learn to fly more than kites now. Finally, like so many mothers of that time, Bertha was resigned to her son's military service: "Now until the war is over and the Stars and Stripes fly again over all free territory that is now in enemy hands, we must loan you to Uncle Sam--and pray for your safe return."

At Santa Ana, the cadets underwent more testing, physical fitness, and drill. The Army selected Ozzie to help with drill practice as he knew this from high school and college R.O.T.C. He also underwent a strict physical examination and passed; many other cadets did not. He pulled his share of "army" duties, attended classes, and wrote home as often as possible. In his initial letters, he optimistically predicted that the war would be over in a matter of a few months. Events proved otherwise.

On May 27, he left for Sequoia Field, Visalia, California, to begin Primary Flight School. In those days, a pilot's training consisted of three phases, each lasting about two months; each was progressively more difficult and challenging. The first was primary flight training. Ozzie in a May 29 letter to Herschel Bricker described his new environment as "a wonderful place compared with anything I've seen in the Army yet. We sleep in walnut beds--no more army cots--and we have walnut desks and chairs for studying etc. The food is like something you'd get in a Florida hotel and it's just a grand set-up in general." He heard from his Masque friend

Earle Rankin and had a visit from Norman Mennes whom he knew while at Maine. In 1941, Bricker hired Mennes to help with scenery and technical production for the Maine Masque. He was from Santa Ana, California. This helped Austin stay connected to his past and his love for theater. He was happy.

Meanwhile, Earle Rankin pulled a prank on Ozzie as he explained in a June 8, 1942 letter to Herschel Bricker: "I got a letter from Ozzie the other day and he told me about his transfer; he seems much happier there. I wrote him a mess of bull about how Gwen Cushing was ga-ga over him and I expect that I'll be hearing from Gwen soon giving me the devil again!" Gwen played opposite Austin as Flora in *Jim Dandy*. Later, in this same letter, Rankin said: "Got a letter from Ozzie again and he's just wild over all the goo I poured in his ear about Gwen! I must cook up some more before I write again." Austin wasn't quite the fool that Earle thought, however. Shortly thereafter, Ozzie wrote to Bricker: "I got a grand letter from Earle yesterday ...he just spent most of ...three pages telling me about Gwen! ...I'm being matched up with Gwen. Can't say that I'd mind. She's a swell person. I certainly enjoyed that Jim Dandy bit with her. She's very easy to play to!" Austin and Gwen were corresponding as Masque friends but now his letters became more impassioned and frequent. One such letter Austin never sent to Gwen quotes lines from *Jim Dandy*, as "Don't go (Gwen)-I-I'm too far from too many things already--Stay awhile! Stay." Bricker got wind of this caper and put an end to it. Gwen acknowledged her gratefulness to him in a July 15 letter, but assured him that she and Austin remained friends: "He's an awfully nice friend, and I wouldn't say anything abrupt to hurt him for worlds." Austin soon forgot this joke; he was too busy learning to fly and preparing for war. He and Earle remained friends, a tribute to his magnanimous and forgiving character.

By mid June, Ozzie was taking to the air. The Army Air Forces used the Ryan PT-22 Recruit airplane for primary flight training. Built by the same St. Louis company that made Charles Lindbergh's Spirit of St. Louis, the PT-22 was ideally suited for beginning pilots. The aircraft was powered by a five-cylinder Kinner engine that moved the machine at a top speed of 120 mph. A two-seater, the instructor sat in the front while the student sat in the rear. Ozzie made progress with his flying and toward the end of June he soloed for the first time. He described this milestone in a letter to Bricker: "I soloed last week--yes--it was quite a thrill to get a plane up there alone and then have to land it. (A mighty queer sensation not to see that instructor's head in the front cockpit.) I now have about 16 1/2 hours total flying time and usually fly about 2 hours per day." The Army appointed Ozzie a cadet officer after a stiff competition; he was placed second in command of his company. As part of his new duties, he assisted the flight training officers to acclimate the new class of air cadets or "dodos." He remained optimistic about the war coming to a quick close, and he now looked at being drafted as a good event in his life for it helped him to understand life more fully.

As if Ozzie were not busy enough, he volunteered to be the editor of his class's yearbook. But that was just like him to be always doing something, and it gave him a chance to use writing skills that he developed in high school and honed while at the university. He titled the yearbook *Prop Wash, 42K, July 1942, Sequoia Field*. It chronicled the first-time flying experiences of 250 flight cadets and described the daily routines of the first stage of flight training. For those who "washed out" or failed as many did and then were reassigned

34 a

Front Cover: *42-K Prop Wash, July 1942, Sequoia Field*

elsewhere, he graciously gave them credit in a short piece called Company E: " From upper class, from lower class, from all companies, A to D, come men to Co. E. E could stand for end--it doesn't; it could stand for elimination (members of E Co. maintain that it doesn't); E could stand for exclusive--and the more philosophical members of the Co. maintain that it does."

Toward the end of July, Ozzie moved on to the second level of pilot education known as basic flight training. He had made "the first of three mileposts and am well on my way," was how he described his progress in a July 30 letter to Bricker. Ozzie relocated to Merced Army Flying School at Merced, California, about 120 miles east of San Francisco. Here the planes were much larger than the Ryans used in primary training. The aircraft was the BT13, a two-seat trainer with a fixed landing gear that was manufactured by Consolidated Vultee. The engine had 450 horsepower, four times the power of the Ryan, and the plane flew at over 160 mph. No wonder Austin was thrilled. Still, he admitted to being "lonesome and blue" when he thought of his friends back at Maine.

Austin took naturally to the air. After only six hours of dual flying instruction, he was among the first of his class to fly solo in the BT13. He adapted quickly to new aircraft types, a facility that allowed him to eventually pilot the most complex aircraft of World War II--the B-29 Superfortress. Later instruction included cross-country navigation and day and night formation flying. He wrote to Bricker and described formation flying as "my idea of fun." World War II pilots needed to master the techniques of formation flying for mutual self-defense over enemy territory. Formation flying also allowed air crews to drop their bombs with pinpoint accuracy, a basic tenet of precision bombing held at that time by the USAAF.

Austin successfully completed the two months of Basic Flight Training by the end of September. Before moving on to Advanced Flight Training, the last stage of his pilot schooling, he visited the Pasadena Playhouse. There he saw Maxwell Anderson's new play, *The Eve of St. Mark*. In a September 27 letter to Bricker, he described his excitement and thought nostalgically of the Maine Masque theater. In this letter, he even drew a sketch of the set and labeled each section so that his theater professor could visualize its unique design. Only one year earlier, Ozzie was at Maine and fully immersed in the activities of the Masque. How quickly world events had changed his life and that of millions of other young Americans. His next stop was Luke Field, Phoenix, Arizona.

Ozzie was now in the last stage of his pilot's training. He had worked hard and had come far. He admitted, though, in a letter to Bricker, that he was a little nervous: "I'm hoping to God everything goes well and something doesn't happen to wash me out." In this same letter, he revealed some of his outlook on life and the war. Apparently, Herschel, in a recent letter, admitted to Ozzie that he felt some discouragement about the Masque back at Maine that fall. Ozzie, though, was quick to reassure him with his optimistic view: "It will all come out right somehow. Fate has funny ways of doing things! We must look for the bright side, even if there doesn't seem to be one. It could be lots worse than it is!" These were encouraging words for one who was preparing himself as an air warrior and for an uncertain future. About the war, Ozzie said:"It will all be over before long and the world can all go back to a fairly normal routine, and everyone can be reunited with their families and friends--that's about all we have to look forward to--in fact that's what we're fighting for! Some of us won't come back but they'll be the ones that made it possible for any of the boys to go home again. So let's just look to that future that we can even now see barely at the horizon!"

In reality, 1942 to date was a dismal year for American war efforts. While the U.S. Navy crippled the Japanese fleet in the battles of the Coral Sea and Midway, the Japanese land forces remained entrenched across thousands of square miles in the Far East. Just off the east coast, German submarines sank American ships with impunity while in Europe, Nazi armies pushed Russian forces back to the gates of Moscow itself. And still no American forces were on the European continent. But like the soothsayer of his high school days, Ozzie saw into the future with his positive outlook.

At Luke Field, Ozzie flew the most sophisticated and challenging aircraft yet, the North American Harvard AT-6. Equipped with a 550hp Pratt and Whitney radial engine, this plane, with collapsible landing gear, reached over 200 mph. As before, Ozzie adapted quickly to the new and more powerful machine while growing more confident in his piloting skills.

As he had done at Sequoia, Ozzie volunteered at Luke Field to be the editor of his class's cadet book titled simply *Luke Field, Class 42K*. It was a special yearbook, though, because Ozzie arranged for the Walt Disney Studios to draw cartoons for placement throughout the book. The Disney Studios produced a total of 19 original cartoons that featured Donald Duck in a number of caricatures of air cadet life. This yearbook was a larger more detailed work than the one at Sequoia and allowed Ozzie to insert some meaningful and sensitive prose. A dedication, for example, stated: "We fondly dedicate this book to those whose thoughts and prayers have meant so much to us--our parents and loved ones--may we be an honor to them in the greater endeavor ahead."

Ozzie also wrote an essay at the end of the Luke Field yearbook. This essay highlights the transformative experience that flight training was for him and for other young American men preparing to fight in World War II:

> Some few months ago, the Class of 42-K stepped forth with its left foot, in proper military style, and began the long training period required to become pilots in the United States Army Air Forces. We were a true cross-section of American youth, inexperienced for the most part, but all overflowing with anticipation and more than eager to embark upon what we hoped would be a great and fascinating adventure.
>
> In the beginning, the Air Force seemed to offer a glamorous aspect of life. Thoughts of "the wild blue yonder" and "silver wings" were uppermost in our minds. The glory of the Air Force---Aviation Cadets---the cream of the crop---to us of 42-K there was, without a doubt, nothing like it.
>
> The first thorn in our bed of roses presented itself all too soon. Thunderheads appeared and obstacles blocked our path at regular and irregular intervals, and most of us became a little dubious about all the glory and sunshine among which we had pictured ourselves. From that first moment of doubt, our lives began a series of changes, not drastic at first, but definitely changes. Right there began the long, uphill grind; one of tedious toil, a strenuous day to day

struggle to hold our places in the ranks of ambitious, would-be pilots. Naturally, at first, we were a little shocked, dismayed and greatly disillusioned as our dreams were shattered, but recovery was quick, though not complete, and our determination was aroused. More obstacles came and were surmounted, somehow only adding spice to the struggle. Working under pressure seemed to bring out the best in us. It was very apparent to us all just how wrong our first impressions had been and became even more evident as many of our buddies slipped and fell by the wayside. Realization was, of course, a slow process but we had reached a definite turning point.

We went on to learn a new language---new mannerisms---a new mode for living. Our very characters were reshaped. We now found joy in the satisfaction of accomplishment instead of mere thrills of false pride. Gradually a little of the tension was released as everything was taken in stride and we even began to enjoy our rejuvenated existence to some extent.

As our training reached the last stage, the importance of what we were doing became more and more apparent, and our places were clearly established. Being a part of this country's Air Force began really to mean something to us---each pilot a gear in the finest fighting machine in the world. Those "silver wings" now stood for the sacred emblem of a great group of men. For us to be finally accepted by this select fraternity seems the most natural and yet the greatest of all our accomplishments. "Proud" doesn't seem the right word, for this feeling goes much deeper.

The change-over is complete---the cadet stage is past. Now we stand here at our goal, our first success behind us and look momentarily across the threshold toward a new and greater adventure. We feel that this time we have the typical and proper spirit at the outset. From a group of star-struck, day-dreaming American boys whose HEADS had been full of idle curiosity, wild ideas, and glamorous thought, has been forged a band of keen-minded young American men whose HEARTS are full of the true fighting spirit of the Air Force---the last graduating class of 1941---the Class of 42-K.

One thing we ask; may God grant us His blessings.

Ozzie's advanced flight training progressed quickly, and he remained busy. He was the top man in his section for skeet shooting; a skill used to develop a pilot's gunnery skills. In his spare time, he rode horses over the western wilds that surrounded the airfield. Yet, his thoughts frequently returned to the University of Maine and its Masque Theatre. He assured Bricker, in an early November letter, that he would return. Ozzie expressed this sentiment more strongly in his next November letter to Professor Bricker:" How often I've dreamed at night about being back at Maine in the Little Theatre or in the office, and how blue I've been when I woke up. It's a mighty queer sensation, I tell you. But my one consolation is that someday I'll be coming back to work with you...that is if I live through the war, and if not--I won't be worrying about it--or anything else." With this letter, Ozzie began to ponder his own mortality. And he began to share his apprehension with his professor: "My only fear, as far as <u>fear</u> is concerned, is coming back with only one leg or one arm or with half my face gone!" He felt that a major injury would

Austin Rodney Keith, Cadet 243, 42-K

inhibit his opportunity to act. And he went on to say that he had now "suffered some, had lots of experience, learned a lot about people and places--the world in general and, well, I just feel a deeper understanding of life"--ingredients that he felt made him a better actor.

Ozzie graduated from The West Coast Training Center, United States Army Air Forces on Thursday, December 3, 1942. He earned his commission as a second lieutenant and his wings. He reflected on this accomplishment for him and for his classmates in the essay he wrote for the Luke Field cadet book. In turn, Ozzie's classmates complimented him when they remembered him as a "great flier and something of an editor, this book being his current product."

For his first assignment, Ozzie requested heavy bombers. Instead, the AAF assigned him to the Training Command. He was now a flight instructor himself. He was disappointed but resigned himself to the prospect. "I suppose I'll get used to the idea, but right now I'm a little disgusted. Perhaps I should have been a little less accurate in my flying. If I'd messed it up once in awhile, perhaps they wouldn't think me good enough to teach cadets to fly, but no, I had to do it up brown--always trying my hardest," Ozzie told Bricker in his mid-December letter.

Ozzie did not get home that Christmas, but instead attended a month-long flight instructor's school at Mather Field near San Francisco. During this period, Ozzie was hospitalized for a week due to an infected cut on his neck. He wrote an one act play to help him pass the time away while he recovered. He titled his play, *Prelude To Courage*. Soon, though, he had his assignment: Merced Army Flying School, Merced, California.

By early February, Ozzie was back at Merced. He felt that it was an ironic twist that he was back at the same field where he completed his basic flight training. This time, though, he was an instructor not a student. He predicted that he would be there for at least a year, and that by then the war would be over. America's military progress against its enemies, however, was painfully slow. The Pacific island-hopping campaign begun last August 1942 by the U.S. Marines at Guadalcanal proved slow and costly. The Japanese fiercely held their ground against the Americans. In Africa, the United States forces landed in November to aid the British against Rommel. But Rommel was still full of fight and the tortuous battle for Kasserine Pass was about to begin. Progress against the Nazis was torpid. The Eighth Air Force based in England had just started its precision bombing campaign over the German heartland.

The worst was yet to come. Ozzie pined for home and the theater at Maine. "Lord, how I do wish this war would end and we could all get back to our normal lives again," he wrote in an early February 1943 letter to Bricker. Young and ambitious, he envisioned his future career in theater. Unlike Rosencrantz, who held "ambition of so airy and light a quality that it is but a shadow's shadow," Ozzie had plans.

Chapter Five

More of the Same

> "Together we shall be,
> we shall beget, and begone
> ...Neither art nor science
> nor religion nor poetry
> supports our faith in this action,
> this longing for
> continuity and meaning."
>
> Johnny in *Jim Dandy*
> played by Austin Rodney Keith
> The Maine Masque Theatre, December 17, 18, 1941
> The University of Maine

Ozzie's life at Merced quickly became routine. Each day was filled with flying instruction of new cadets. Ozzie was part of Squadron I, a group of eight 2nd lieutenant instructors all chosen, like himself, out of Advanced Flight Training. Ozzie rated his students on a scale of 1 (low) to 5 (high) on 12 qualities: leadership, judgment, responsibility, military bearing, initiative, self-confidence, force of character, alertness, comprehension, co-operativeness, attention to duty, and professional proficiency. Then, Ozzie averaged these values for an overall score.

Ozzie's correspondence with Herschel Bricker continued uninterrupted. He finally heard from Earle Rankin, his college friend and fellow "Masquer." And he was surprised to hear that the government had called Earle to serve in the armed forces. He wrote to Bricker and expressed his shock that Earle was now in the Army. At least Earle had a chance to finish his degree because of an accelerated special program instituted by the university. Ozzie expressed his appreciation, though, for President Hauck's effort to secure a deferment for him when he was drafted so that he too might move toward completing his degree. Right now, finishing his degree would have to wait. In a November 7, 1942 letter to Charles E. Crossland, Executive Secretary of the Alumni Association, Ozzie assured him that "...I'll be back someday to finish even if I'm 40 (and I probably will be)."

Bricker was attentive in his letters to his former students and encouraged them to pursue their theatrical dreams and potentials despite the war. And Ozzie was one of Bricker's favorites. In response to one such letter, Ozzie wrote on March 13: "It's not what you said, nor is it exactly the way you said it. In fact, I'm not quite sure what it is! It's not that you said I this and I that, even though it does make one feel nice to get a little praise now and then! No--it's just--the letter itself--it was a beautiful mood in an envelope--a mood that left me feeling so--well--'out of this world' is a good typical modern description of it!...At any rate, you surely have given me added incentive to carry on as planned and return to the work I love so well at the earliest possible moment. And beyond that, it becomes much easier to carry on here with all that in view for me in the future. Even so--it's still far over the horizon and there's much work to be done 'before we reach port'!" Bricker's most recent letter had given Ozzie "A touch of happiness, by God!"

But Ozzie's initial optimism that the war would end soon began to change. As 1942 dragged on into 1943 and American casualties rose, he began to be discouraged about the possible length of the war. The longer the war went on, the longer he would be removed from the theatrical world. When Oz-

Squadron I at Merced

zie thought back to his days in the Masque: "I get so enthusiastic only to have it all fade away, my thirst for some theater still not quenched; but, merely--for the time being, 'squelched'! It's pretty discouraging at times and I get that old blue feeling every now and then." The war news carried few stories of allied victories, and the Axis powers remained strong.

Within himself, Ozzie was seeking some deeper answers to life's meaning and purpose. He always believed in God, but really didn't think too much about his belief or faith. But now he began to attend chapel regularly at Merced, and he came to know the airfield's chaplain, Rev. Harold Blakely. As a child, he attended Columbia Street Baptist Church in Bangor with his parents, but he was never baptized. Ozzie now sought baptism. On April 23, 1943, Chaplain Blakely baptized Ozzie and received him into the Methodist Episcopal Church. The simple service that Good Friday centered on the Baptismal Covenant, the Lord's Prayer, The Apostles' Creed, and The Ten Doctrines of Grace.

Ozzie's faith was pragmatic. In early May 1943 he wrote to Bricker and stated that he believed God was in control: "If the Almighty sees fit...he'll take care of it, you can depend on Him." More than a year later in the war, he spoke of "letting Fate handle things..." as a "proper philosophy...I find it very comforting when I can bring myself around to following it." At times he referred to a God-directed fate as "What will come-will come!..." an expression he used in a January 11, 1943 letter to Bricker.

Ozzie's assignment changed by the first of May. He was sent to Carlsbad, New Mexico to learn how to fly twin-engined planes and then to fly bombardier and navigator students on their training missions. As before, he quickly adapted to the new aircraft even though a twin-engined airplane was much different than what he was used to. There, Ozzie flew the Beechcraft AT-11, a specially adapted aircraft with a transparent nose for bombardier training and a plexiglas dome in the roof for navigator celestial training. At the same time he adjusted to the environment of New Mexico, so different from any place he had known before. He spent his free time outdoors horseback riding and hunting in the sage around the airbase. His schedule changed by the end of the month however, when he flew more frequently as the number of bombardier students increased dramatically to meet the AAF war needs. Then that late spring, he left for home on his first leave since entering the service.

Ozzie's leave refreshed him. Not only did he spend time with his family but he got to visit with Herschel Bricker at the University of Maine. He expressed his happiness in a June 28 letter to Bricker for "Such grand talks with you. I'll thrive on the memory for months until I can get back there again...." On the way back to New Mexico, he stopped in New York City to visit with Norman Mennes. Norman was in the Signal Corps Photographic Center stationed in Long Island City. There, in the Big Apple, he and Ozzie saw some shows, met some theatrical people, and toured a film studio. Norman summarized his visit with Ozzie when he wrote to Bricker in July: "I' don't think I've written to you since Austin was here. We had such fun...Ozzie and I saw *Something For The Boys*. That evening, to make us really theatrical, we saw *The Skin Of Our Teeth*, now with Hopkins, of course--and the Fred Waring broadcast. Gwen Anderson had dinner with us so he did meet a Broadway actress. The next morning he came out to the studio with me and I showed him about. I think he enjoyed seeing how pictures are made and I know I enjoyed seeing him, but I wished he could have stayed longer." Ozzie's whirlwind visit east ended when he returned back to Carlsbad at 2 a.m., Saturday, June 26.

Ozzie had four dozen letters waiting for him when he returned to base. Some were from Earle. Their correspondence had increased since Earle was now in the Army Air Forces; they had even more in common these days. In a July 4th letter to Bricker, Rankin expressed his feelings toward Ozzie: "Ozzie is a grand scout and a solid friend--I like him! God protect him."

Soon Ozzie was back to a busy flying schedule. Yet, he reflected on his visit back to his beloved Maine in his next letter to Bricker. "My blood has been replenished with 'Theater Corpuscles' and I ache for the stage...." Ozzie also expressed amusement when Bricker at first did not recognize him when he was home: "I'll never forget the look on your face as I stood there in the doorway of Runion's office! You didn't even know me for 4 or 5 seconds. And what an amazing look came over your features when you finally did recognize me!"

Meanwhile, the momentum of the war built up that summer. U.S. forces launched a campaign against the Japanese in New Georgia. The U.S. and British armies assaulted Sicily in what was the beginning of an end to Italy's collusion with Nazi Germany. The foray into the "soft underbelly" of Europe, though, would prove tortuous and costly for the Allies. German forces launched massive tank attacks against Soviet forces on the open plains of the Ukraine. But for Ozzie, life was once again routine with training bombardier and navigator students and assisting in other assigned duties. Ozzie hinted at a little spark in his life in a July 31 letter to Bricker when he said: "I flew over to Phoenix, Ariz. last weekend to 'fan an old flame'! A sweet little girl I knew there when I was a cadet in Advanced Flying School! Have to keep a few on the string so I'll have something to choose from in case I ever get too lonely and decide I need a mate, which, incidentally, is the <u>farthest</u> thing from my mind right now!" He also hinted that he might have a chance to do some radio drama at Carlsbad. He hoped to write scripts. A shortage of wire for the radio studio, though (not an unusual occurrence during WWII), held up the project. As before, he actively sought out opportunities to use his writing and theatrical skills.

Over that long hot summer, Ozzie expressed boredom in a letter to his friend Earle. He also began to worry about his future place in the world of theater. He longed for his past days in the Maine Masque: "I love the Masque and all it stands for so very much, it's hard to express it in words...It's simply my whole life....nothing...means as much to me as getting back to Maine and the Masque and sinking my teeth into some heavy drama! And I do mean <u>heavy</u>! Some days, I feel as though I could play the deepest-heaviest-grandest part ever written--and to perfection! I get the urge so often, but can only let it fizzle out!" For the time being, he would have to content himself with the radio project at Carlsbad.

Ozzie continued to receive letters from Norman and Earle and from another Masquer he knew at Maine, Maynard French. These helped him stay connected with theater. And, by September, he had enough wire for his radio project but still lacked a control booth in which to produce radio shows. The carpenters never showed up, but he was a doer. So he and the others involved built the studio themselves. He had the help of four enlisted men, a WAC, and a female civilian, but he was the only officer. He marveled at his carpentry skills when he wrote to Bricker in September. Ozzie also thought that "This 'radio' will tide me over...It's far from the 'real Mc'Coy' but there's a slight tang of theater there." So, in his words, life was "pretty bearable right now."

By mid-October, the radio station was up and running. Ozzie was having a great deal of fun ad libbing etc. It was "Lacking that certain something..." he thought. In a late October letter, he also told his former professor that he would be home on another leave in early November and to expect a visit. He wished that his friends from his Maine Masque days who were now in the armed forces could also have a leave at the same time so that they could have a "Grand old fashioned reunion, including a bit of acting or reading or something. How I yearn for it!" But that was not to be.

Ozzie's November leave passed rapidly. He visited with his family in Bangor, of course, and visited with Herschel in his Orono apartment. "It was grand getting back there..." he wrote on November 26 to Bricker, "Certainly enjoyed our short visit together too, and I can still taste that delicious salad 'your own little hands' threw together for supper my last night there!" In this same letter, he humorously described his trip back to New Mexico. From Dow Field he flew in an Army plane to Manchester, N.H., changed planes and flew on to Boston. Then he took a train to New York City where he was able to get a ride in a bomber to Chicago. From there, he took the train to Denver and then flew with Continental Airlines to Carlsbad. He was in New York long enough to take in a Broadway production titled *Harriet* with Helen Hayes. Also this month, the Army Air Forces promoted him to First Lieutenant.

Once back, Ozzie's flying schedule increased and soon another Christmas passed. His correspondence with his professor diminished and Herschel expressed concern. Ozzie responded to his professor's worries with reassurances in a January 23, 1944 letter: "I still love Maine, the state, the university and especially the Masque." He attributed his lack of writing to laziness, but he also admitted to being in love with "My little Spanish Beauty...." Ozzie appreciated Bricker's fatherly concern when he had not heard from him for two months. Ozzie also mentioned in this letter that Earle Rankin was in training to become a bombardier, and that the chances for Earle to be stationed at Carlsbad were very good as the AAF was centralizing all bombardier training there. Earle even hoped to have Ozzie as an instructor. Time would tell. In the same letter, Ozzie promised to write again regularly and that, "I'm always waiting for the moment when I can return there to stay! As Earle so quaintly put it-'I fly with Klieg lights in my eyes.'"

The radio programming at Carlsbad continued to go well and it gave Ozzie a chance to stay involved in theater. He and his small group of radio volunteers received congratulations from all sectors of Carlsbad Army Air Field for their shows. Yet, as the war continued, he once again expressed concern in a February 5 letter to Bricker that his talent was getting rusty. "I'm wondering if I'm losing the touch, the feel of it! I guess that's a natural fear after one is away from it for awhile!...I'm not really terrified by the thought, but it does haunt me a little at times!"

Later that February, Ozzie told Bricker that his radio group may perform the play *Seven Keys to Baldpate* live, and that he would direct. By early March, he had his cast and rehearsals were underway. He also, much to his surprise, had a foray into acting at Carlsbad when an off-base community theater

Ozzie at Carlsbad with his 1936 Buick

group contacted him for help with a play they were doing. A lead character, a soldier, transferred, and they needed a replacement. Ozzie admitted to Bricker in a March 1944 letter, that the play group: "Worked on my ego, speaking to the effect that they thought with my experience et. cetera, and like the moron I am, I said I'd try anything once. This should be a laugh to you--<u>me</u>-- who never knew his lines till the last week of rehearsals--learning the whole play in one day--but somehow I did it." The play went well, and the group called Ozzie a "God--send"! This flurry of theatrical activity bolstered Ozzie; he felt elated. This reemergence into theater for Ozzie, however, did not last long.

The year 1943 had been a critical one for the war efforts of the United States. American industry turned out an abundance of military equipment and trained millions to meet the manpower quotas of the military. The next year, 1944, would be crucial for the United States as it sought to turn its industrial might and abundant manpower against its enemies. In Europe, America with its allies, would launch a daring frontal attack from England eastward onto mainland Europe while Soviet forces from the east, pushed the Nazi juggernaut back. The AAF would step up its bombing campaign against Nazi industry and seek air control over the continent. In the vast Pacific area, American forces would pick up the pace of island hopping to take back the Philippines and to move toward Japan itself despite tremendous resistance by the Japanese. And bombing of Japan by America's new super bomber, the B-29 from bases in China would begin. American casualties would reach the highest level for any of the war years. For Ozzie,1944 would be a crucial year too. He would prepare for combat, and become a player in the greatest drama Earth had yet seen--World War II. This year he would also enter his one act play, *Prelude to Courage,* into a play contest at the University of Maine.

Ozzie's play deals with the fear of death and its uncertainty-- the nemesis of all warriors-- whether this fear is conscious or unconscious. Ozzie's play is a statement of his faith and how the power of this faith allows him to overcome his fear. And what better way for Ozzie to express this human message than through theater. Theater along with his faith, gives Ozzie fulfillment and meaning thus contradicting the lines he spoke as Johnny in *Jim Dandy*:

> "Together we shall be, we shall beget, and begone...Neither art not science nor religion nor poetry supports our faith in this action, this longing for continuity and meaning."

Chapter Six

The Play

Prelude to Courage

by

Austin R. Keith

Scene: Small auditorium at an Air Forces Advanced Flying School. At the back of the stage is a small platform about two feet high with three chairs and a speakers stand, all facing the audience. Dark backdrops in back and at sides. American flag at right of stand and other flag at left. In foreground are several rows of chairs with backs to audience and facing platform. Two steps leading up to platform from either side. Other scenery and props may be included in keeping with the Army Air Forces.

Time: A day the last of July 1942, shortly before sunset. It is graduation day for a class of Aviation Cadets.

Curtain Rises

to reveal.......

Steve Brown standing in the center of the aisle which runs from the speakers platform down between the rows of chairs to apron. Steve is downstage near the last row of seats and facing right as if looking out the window; but obviously deep in thought and seeing nothing. Steve is of normal stature, a little slender, fair of skin; and healthy looking. He is dressed in an officer's uniform with 2nd Lt's rank, and pilot's wings on the left breast. He had just received his wings and commission earlier that day. In his hand he holds a hat. He turns slowly to the floor...at this moment enter Joe Phillips and Bob Joyce, from downstage left. Bob is a sturdy boy, about six feet tall, the football type...full of fun but not rowdy. Joe is slightly smaller but also well built and very good looking. Bob and Joe have been close pals since college days and Steve a good friend of the two who knew them at college. Both Bob and Joe also are dressed as Steve is and have graduated that day. When they are a few feet inside the door they notice Steve and hesitate slightly before crossing to him. They have all come to the auditorium for the same reason namely to take a last look at the place where they had the thrill of receiving their wings. The two cross to Steve who hasn't noticed until they speak........

JOE: Hello Steve...old man..we've er..a..been looking for you.
BOB: Hi Steve.
STEVE: (Startled and slightly embarrassed) Oh...Oh...hi fellas (Embarrassed pause) I...er...a...I just dropped in here. (trying to make up an excuse for his being there)
BOB: (Interrupting and trying also to make an excuse for his and Joe's presence) Ah...Joe and I left our...er...

a...a...programs here and we thought we might be able to.....

JOE: (Interrupting) Oh hell...you two... we all know why we're here so why be coy and make all these pretensions. We're just three sentimental old fools, and somehow...I'm not ashamed of it. (There is a moment of silence as Bob looks a little meek and uneasy)

BOB: (Grinning) Yeah...I guess that's about it. Couldn't bear to leave here without taking one more look at the place where we had the biggest thrill of our lives.

JOE: That word "thrill," my friends is a masterpiece of understatement.

STEVE: It certainly was a big day, wasn't it. One we won't forget as long as...as long as we...live (faintly) (Joe looks a little puzzled but smiles and rushes into his next line.)

JOE: Say Steve, where are you going...what did you pull down?

STEVE: Oh...I...I'm leaving tomorrow for Guadalcanal... guess...I'm going to fly P-38's...yes...leaving tomorrow. (Pensively)

BOB: Oh Steve so soon...boy that's tough..I don't envy you.

STEVE: Yeah...I know.

JOE: (Hastily) Bob and I are still going to be together, Steve, isn't that great. We're on orders to go to four engine transition school. We ship out of there to phase training...and then...England here we come.

STEVE: (Earnestly pleased) Oh say that's swell. I'm so glad you two didn't get separated. You've been buddies for so long, it would be a shame to split you up now. You've both been sweating it out more than you'd care to have anyone know, haven't you? (Bob and Joe look at each other with sheepish grins) Phillips and Joyce what a combination. (They all laugh)

JOE: (Laughing) Steve, this lug and I have been pals so long that we're actually beginning to look and act alike.

BOB: God forbid.

JOE: Stop stealing my lines Lieutenant. (Bob gives him a farcical salute)

JOE: As I was about to say, before the untimely interruption (a dirty look at Bob who winces with the pain of it) we are so much alike that I get most of his demerits when he gets out of line.

BOB: (Roughing him up) the hell you say...who was it that walked tours on the ramp all last Sunday afternoon ...I've still got blisters on my feet. (They all try to keep up their spirits with a little horseplay. This is the parting of the ways for a long time perhaps forever. It's working on Steve...he's losing the moodiness and beginning to be himself again...he smiles as Bob and Joe go at it.)

JOE: (Out from under an arm) Why...they even handed me Bob's diploma at graduation. (They all laugh again as Bob lets Joe go.)

STEVE: Outside of old Walrus Face's speech that was the best part of the whole affair. (Warming up to the horseplay. In a loud voice as if reading from a paper) Lt. Joseph Phillips...(laughing) and then when you stand up he hands you your diploma and says 'Congratulations Lt. Joyce,' Boy did that bring the house down.

BOB: Oh but the Colonel's speech was the tops. That man doesn't know it but he should be in burlesque.

JOE: It wouldn't surprise me any if he had been at one time.

STEVE: Completely himself again, moodiness gone...personality plus...hurries down the aisle, jumps up on the platform laying his cap on a chair he turns and faces the front and in a commanding voice) Gentlemen...take seats. (Bob and Joe seeing they are to take part in a farce and eager to keep up their spirits step to the back row and sit down stiffly at attention, arms folded high up on their chests.)

STEVE: May I now present the commandant of the field...Colonel Walrus face...I mean the distinguished Colonel Hilton. Colonel Hilton. (Steve turns away then walks back to the rostrum as Colonel Hilton, stroking an Imaginary Walrus Mustache,) (His voice is guttural and harsh as...

STEVE: (As Colonel Hilton) Hrrumph! (Bursts of laughter from Bob and Joe) You may be at ease. (Bob and Joe exaggerate relaxing) Hrrumph! (Another giggle from Bob and Joe) Gentlemen of the graduating class, Ladies and Gentlemen, Guests and Friends, we are gathered here today...we are er...a...gathered here today (breaks out of character by change of voice) Does anyone dare deny that? (Back in character) We are gathered here today to celebrate rather to...to...to (Break in Character) to bid...do I hear three...who bids three...going at two, going, once...Sold! to the bald headed gentlemen in the pink pajamas. (Back in Character) We are gathered here today (Break in Character) Monotonous isn't it? (Mimicking Jerry Colonel)

STEVE: (Back in character) Hmmm...I've lost the blooming place. (Pantomimes looking through sheets for paper) Blast the bloody notes. (Pantomimes throwing three more over his shoulder) Hrumph...this is a great occasion...we have here a group of young men who in my opinion are typical young Americans ..and although we have had our differences at times and they have not always conducted themselves in the best manner...the L-i-t-t-l-e d-e-v-i-l-s....they have on the whole done a fine job. (Lights start slow fade representing fading light at sunset)

BOB: (Shouting out) You're right!

STEVE: Thank you friend (an aside to the audience) my stooge. (Stroking mustache) Hrrumph...which reminds me of a little story I heard when I was a fighter in the last world war. It seems a bunch of the boys were whooping it up in one of those yokon halls...oh good gracious no...ah...er...a...as I was saying...these boys have been working hard for several months learning to fly, learning to shoot, learning to become fine future officers. Tomorrow they will be a part of the greatest fighting machine in the world. (Towards the end of that speech Steve has dropped out of character and is now speaking in his own voice with that far-away look in his eyes again. He is almost preaching here) They will go overseas in their mighty mechanical battle steeds and win glory for themselves and their country. They will blast the enemy from the skies, blast them from the seas, blast them from the land...blasted to hell. (Bob and Joe look at each other uneasily) (Steve suddenly comes to and gets back in character.) Hrrumph...from this very room may come a Washington, a Lee, a Grant, a Pershing, or maybe two or three of each...we're easily satisfied. (Bob and Joe laugh again) (In a loud voice Steve announces) Forty years later. (Then a change of character to himself forty years later) My friends...now that we have declared war on Bermuda...I...General Brown...four stars, wish to introduce my staff. General Phillips also four stars, chief operations on the eastern front. (By this time Joe and Bob are on the platform bowing profoundly in all directions.)

STEVE: (Mimicking Jimmy Durante) Everybody wants to get in de act.

BOB: And at this time I should like to introduce my staff. Here on my left is my right hand man Col. Yehudi (Indicating thin air)...better known as to the spiritual world as...the Ghost of Johnny Emerson. (Joe looks sharply at him as does Steve)

STEVE: (At the breaking point suddenly)--Did you have to say that? (He jumps down from the platform and goes to the back row of chairs and sits facing stage right his head hanging) (Bob and Joe look at each other and Bob shrugs as they move down to Steve)

BOB: Jeez Steve, (Pause) I guess I just didn't ---think. I should---well---someone ought to take a poke at me. (Emphatically)

STEVE: (Without looking up reaches out and squeezes Bob's arm) Aw---forget it fella---I'm sorry I let myself go that way.

JOE: (Pulling up a chair from across the aisle and facing the front) (He sits down along-side Steve.) We're all under such a nervous strain that things get under our skins a lot easier that they ordinarily would, Steve.

STEVE: (Looking up and not out over the audience) No Joe---no---that's not it. It's just---well---I saw the plane afterwards---what was left of it. It was black with the exploding gas tanks. There wasn't enough (break in voice)---left of Johnny---to---even--identify him. (Hangs his head again and shakes it as if to clear his mind of the sight.)

BOB: One thing sure, Steve, he never knew what happened---it was all over just like that. (Snaps his fingers)

STEVE: (Doesn't seem to hear Bob) (Looking out over the audience again) He was the best damn roommate a fellow ever had. (A long pause) His folks were on their way down here for graduation and the War Department couldn't reach them in time to stop them. What a shock it must have been to them when they arrived here. Killed the day before graduation ----dead---it just doesn't seem possible---Johnny Emerson---dead. (Hangs head again)
(Lights have pretty well faded by now leaving little light on the stage except a bright light on the rostrum and a faint spot on the boys so that they are practically silhouettes)

JOE: (Rising and gripping Steve's shoulder) It's getting dark Steve, are you coming along to dinner? (Soothingly)

STEVE: (Waving them along) No---no---I'm not very hungry ----you two go ahead. I'll see you later at the BOQ.

JOE: Okay, Steve.

BOB: See ya later, Steve. (Bob and Joe exit downstage left) (Steve turns and faces platform---slumped in chair. He doesn't see an elderly man who enters same door by which Bob and Joe just left and stands gazing at the platform in deep thought. The man is about fifty years old, medium height, heavy set, iron gray hair, small mustache, wearing light conservative summer suit and carrying a light felt hat. The stage is completely dark now except for the bright light on the platform and the faint spot on Steve. Steve turns to his left suddenly with the man at his back and gripping his hands fiercely...and looking up into the spotlight....)

STEVE: Guadalcanal...oh God...I'm afraid...I'm scared...God ...scared stiff. (He drops his head and sobs quietly)

MAN: (He couldn't help overhearing) Don't you think we all are son? (He crosses to Steve and both are now in the faint spot) (His manner is sympathetic)

STEVE: (Turns startled) Oh...you startled me sir...I didn't hear you come in. I.....(slightly embarrassed)

MAN: I didn't mean to intrude...I just sort of stepped in here for a (Pause)...look.

STEVE: (Relieved) Oh...did you come to see your son graduate sir?

MAN: (Hesitatingly)Yes...I...I came to see my son graduate.

STEVE: (Trying to cover up his embarrassment and also be courteous) It certainly has been a big day here. Wish my folks could have been here but they live too far away.

MAN: (Deeply sorry) Oh that's too bad...I wish they could have seen it.

STEVE: They called long distance which was next best to having them here.

MAN: I'll bet they're mighty proud of their son.

STEVE: (Laughing nervously) I guess so. I hope so. Doesn't seem to be much else that matters. (Thoughtful pause) I had a classmate who was killed yesterday when he crashed his plane purposely to avoid hitting another ship with six men in it. His parents should be awfully proud of him. We all are. His name was Johnny Emerson...perhaps you heard about it.

MAN: (With guarded interest and softly) Did you know...

	the...boy...very well?
STEVE:	He..he was my roommate. He..(Steve looks at the man anxiously)
MAN:	Go ahead, son...get it off your chest. (Steve starts to speak...then pauses)
MAN:	Tell me about him...what was he like? (Still quietly and with guarded interest) (He pulls two chairs up and they sit down)
STEVE:	(Starts slowly, dramatically with faraway look) Johnny was one of those fellows who's hard to describe. He was just an ordinary guy....yet as I look back now a very extraordinary guy. He was quiet by nature, yet always ready for fun. He didn't like to fight but if any of his friends were in a good one he was the toughest hombre in the bunch. He'd back a friend down to his last cent...and that goes for the shirt off his back. He was sincere about everything. When he was working at something he worked hard and when he played he played hard. He studied more than anyone I ever knew...he often got demerits for having the lights on after taps...studying. He was the hottest pilot in the class...of...he was just everything you'd want to have all wrapped up in one person. He was Joe America himself. (Long pause) He was the best roommate a fellow ever had. (Man has been eating up every word tears in his eyes and now looks up as if in reverence. Thanking God) And he died the way he lived...being a grand guy...cracking himself up to save a lot of other people. (Pause...then with a break in his voice) But why did he have to die...why...why does a guy like that have to die...God it doesn't seem fair.
MAN:	(Gently and restrainingly) Death is not such a terrible thing as you seem to think, son. It's even been

	known to be pretty beautiful.
STEVE:	Perhaps I'm a coward. I never thought I was...but well I'm afraid of death, terribly afraid.
MAN:	(Very gently but firmly) Listen to me, my boy, it's not death itself you fear...it's the uncertainty of living and dying...the not knowing when or how or where that you fear. If you believe in God and the hereafter, death <u>is</u> beautiful and can be looked forward to rather than dreaded. And I know you do believe, because I heard you speak to God, and only one of faith ever does that. So you see...it's not really death you fear but the uncertainty. And it doesn't take a coward to fear that...only a...a moron doesn't. We are all afraid every day. Our lives are full of fears some small and some great. You surely don't think you are the only one do you? Don't you think your friend...Johnny was afraid in those last seconds before he died.....of course he was. All fear is pretty much alike when you get right down to it...like that feeling of anxiety when you're lining up for the opening kick off of a football game...or perhaps that little sensation in your stomach before some minor operation in a hospital. In the theater it's called stage fright...another place it's called something else....but it's an emotion we all have and none of us can get away from it. Perhaps you think these are poor examples to be comparing with the great fear you have in your heart now, but in reality it's the same thing. Perhaps you think this sounds like too simple an explanation for the tormenting confusion you feel within you. Not <u>too</u> simple, lad...not <u>too</u> simple because....actually it <u>is</u> as simple as that. (He pauses and looks at Steve for a moment) ...<u>You know all great</u> warriors will tell you they are always cold

with fear when they go into battle...One of them once said "A man without fear is a fool!" Then I recall another saying "A man who is never afraid has no emotion and a man without emotion is not a good fighter. Well we need good fighters badly... and, son I have a feeling you're going to be one of the best.

STEVE: (After a slight hesitation) I...I...don't exactly know what to say, sir. You....well... I...I think I understand a lot that I didn't before. I guess I....well...thanks.

MAN: (Smiling and slapping Steve on the shoulder rises) Well....I've got to run along...my wife will be waiting. Just remember, lad, the other fellow...your enemy...will probably be twice as scared as you are.

STEVE: I will sir....and...thanks again.

MAN: (Holding out his hand) What is your name, son?

STEVE: (Shaking hands) Stephen Brown, sir.

MAN: Well goodbye Steve, and....best of luck. (He turns and walks quickly away, but Steve takes a step or two after him and stops him with....)

STEVE: Sir, I'd like to remember your name....but you didn't mention it.

MAN: (Stops, turns half way around so he's facing the audience) Oh...yes...well...my name is Emerson... John Emerson, Sr. (He turns and hurries out a little flustered) (Steve stands and gapes after him, almost unbelieving. Then he goes to the door and looks out after him. He stands there for a moment...then gazes at his wings reflectingly, and walks back to the platform to get his hat. As he comes down off the platform, he pauses as he comes abreast of the American flag, looks at it tenderly almost reverently, and touches it with his left hand very delicately, then turns and moves slowly downstage into the

faint spot and stops facing front)
STEVE: (With tears in his eyes and a half smile on his lips looks up into the spotlight)   Thanks.....Johnny.

----------Slow Curtain----------

Chapter Seven

A Constant Guiding Star

"And I guess no matter what life will do
to him, he can take care of it now..."

Nat Miller, in *Ah Wilderness*
played by Austin Rodney Keith
The Maine Masque Theatre, April 28-May 1, 1941
The University of Maine

Ozzie arrived at Hobbs Army Airfield in eastern New Mexico toward the end of March, 1944. There he would attend a B-17 transition school and learn to fly a four-engined bomber. In a March 30 letter to Herschel Bricker, Ozzie enthusiastically explained his new status: "At last I'm on my way to combat! True--it's only the first step and it'll be awhile yet before I actually see action, but at least I've got out of the training command and into something besides a training plane...I'll be here around eight or nine weeks, I think, then I'm not quite sure where I go. I'm supposed to go to B-29s--that's the new large bomber that hasn't been used in combat yet!" He promised to write to his professor again soon about what he called "his new set-up."

Ozzie did not write Bricker for a month. In the interim, his friend Earle Rankin wrote to Bricker on April 26 and told him that he had heard from Norman Mennes that Ozzie asked for combat. "I don't like that..." Rankin added. Finally, Ozzie wrote to Bricker in late April and gave him an update on his training: "I'm still learning all about everything to do with four-engine ships and doing my share of the flying here. It's pretty much routine now, as it always is after one has done a thing for a short while." But Ozzie did not explain his reason for requesting combat until late that year. Ozzie reasoned in a letter to Bricker just before Christmas: "I'm not bloodthirsty, but I want to do my share, complete my missions and come back to the states without the remorse that I've been carrying inside me ever since I graduated in December of 1942--the feeling that I wasn't really doing my part." Apparently, he confided his feelings to Bricker before because he went on to say: "Silly? Yes, you always told me that...."

No doubt, Ozzie was conscientious and wanted to do his part for the war effort. But by the spring of 1944, the Army Air Forces also approached its two and one-half million man quota. In fact the recruitment of young American men for the Army's air arm was so successful that General Arnold released all aviation trainees who had volunteered from ground or service forces for air crew training in a letter dated 1 April 1944. These aviation trainees now went back to the regular army. General Arnold stated: "The Army Air Forces team has succeeded better than we dared hope for when our quotas were set and it now permits a reduction in our training rate." Training of combat crews continued but at a reduced rate more in tune with need. As a result, the AAF gave pilots within the Training Command an opportunity for combat. Indeed, as the AAF began to select pilots for the B-29, it chose pilots out of the Training Command rather than directly from AAF schools. It was thought that the flying experience of Training Command pilots was crucial for the quick build-up of B-29 bombardment groups.

Ozzie looked at his changed status with typical optimism and good humor:" I'll be so glad to get into a tactical outfit, if for no other reason than to get out of New Mexico and its eternal and infernal wind and sand, " he wrote on April 27. In the same letter, Ozzie longed to return to Maine and the Maine Masque theater and worried that his mentor would not be there after the war: " Lord, I pray that you'll still be at Maine when I do get back. I just want you to know that if you aren't I doubt seriously if I shall ever set foot inside its halls of learning again."

Nearly two months elapsed without word from Bricker. Ozzie was in despair when in a mid-May letter to Herschel he asked "Have you and the Masque disowned and abandoned me?" His life now was " Strictly army till this mess is over... No more recent thrills of delving into theater! I miss hearing from you so damn much." The next day, he received a card from Bricker and on May 19 a letter. His fears were allayed. In his letter back to his professor that day, he declared: "I don't know what I'd ever do if we--you and I-- were to lose sight of each other! I look to you so much for guidance in theater...A constant guiding star--that's you."

Ozzie felt good that his connection to theater and to Maine was still there for him. Then, he asked Bricker if he had seen the play that he sent in for the Maine Masque Theatre Playwriting Contest. He wondered what Bricker thought of it, "Personally! The name was *Prelude to Courage!*" The executive committee of the Maine Masque Theatre issued twelve guidelines for its contest. Entries were due by March 20, 1944, and a three-judge panel would decide the winner. This panel was comprised of a member of the executive committee of the Masque, the director of the Maine Masque Theatre, and an English Department faculty member. Since Ozzie had not heard, he presumed his play wasn't in the running.

As in the past, Ozzie adapted easily to flying what was for

Ozzie at the Controls of a B-29

him a new aircraft, the B-17. Boeing's B-17 and Consolidated's B-24 were the backbone of the Army Air Forces bombing campaigns. A new bomber, Boeing's B-29, now reached ample production and was being deployed to the CBI or the China, Burma, and India war zone. The B-29 was initially conceived in 1940 as a long-range bomber that could reach Nazi Germany from the United States. At that time, it was unclear whether England would survive the Nazi onslaught. Now, at this stage in the war, the B-29 could be used to bomb the Japanese heartland from bases in China. Compared to the B-17, the B-29 was considerably larger and faster; it could carry three times the bomb load.

Ozzie finished the Four-Engine Pilots Transition Course at Hobbs on June 3 and received a diploma. His next stop was the Lincoln Army Air Field in Nebraska where a B-29 transition center was located. Here, he would undergo special teamwork training. Effective teamwork was so essential for the successful operation of the complex B-29. First, though, Ozzie went home on leave.

Everything was in full bloom in Bangor when Ozzie was home in June. He had not been home for seven months, but things had not changed much. He visited relatives and friends but spent as much time as possible with his folks at 10 Boynton Street. People seldom spoke about the war even though all the radio stations carried news accounts of the Allied invasion of France. Soon he was on his way back west but stopped in New York City toward the end of June to see Herschel Bricker who was there on business as President of the American Educational Theater Association. They met at the Hotel Piccadilly. Maynard French, one of Ozzie's friends from the Maine Masque, was also there. They talked theater until late at night, and no doubt Bricker told him that he had won the Masque playwriting contest with his play *Prelude to Courage*. Ozzie was refreshed and alive with theater once again!

Ozzie spent most of July at Lincoln Army Airfield for his B-29 transition training. At Lincoln, an AAF staging area, the Personnel Distribution Command helped personnel transfer-between commands with records, training, physical condition, and qualifications prior to shipment for overseas combat duty. Ozzie was busy with his combat preparation when on July 18, he received the Maine Masque newsletter with a write-up about his play *Prelude to Courage* .

"I got the newsletter today and was quite surprised with the news coverage and no less happy about the whole thing... Gave me a good feeling...," he said in a July 18 letter to Bricker. He also indicated in this letter that he recently dabbled in other art forms in his limited spare time. He made a clay model of a human face: "It wasn't bad for my first attempt." In the literary field, he wrote a short story and planned to send it off to *Colliers Magazine*. And then this brief poem appeared in his letter which, he said, was inspired by "The Enchanted Land", that is New Mexico:

> Oh raging wind and blinding sand
> Oh blazing desert heat
> Stay thy harsh tormenting hand
> I beg, beseech, entreat.
> All ye rampant forces wild
> Hear my pleading cry
> Lest my waning courage fail
> And leave me here to die

But these forays into the arts were brief. "There won't be

much time for art of any kind from now on...I'll be getting ready for combat and shortly afterwards I'll be across." Until he left stateside, though, he continued to try his hand at different art forms when he had some spare moments.

Congratulations for Ozzie's playwriting success came to Herschel in letters from other Maine Masquers. In a tongue in cheek tribute, fellow Bangorean and actor Dayson DeCourcy said in a July 23 letter: "I was amused and amazed to learn that dear 'Ozzie' had done something worthwhile. I guess you know that I probably would have won first honors had I, too, been in the air corps where one has an abundance of 'free' time. Ah, yes, we poor upraised, mud-slogging foot soldiers go on about our many and varied duties not seeking glory, but merely trying to do a job that only we know and appreciate. Seriously, H. L. my heartiest congratulations to Keith--I'd like to read his play." Dayson, now in the Infantry, and Ozzie had appeared in several Masque productions and were sometimes good natured rivals. Lewis Chadwick, another of Ozzie's fellow actors, extended his congratulations and comments on Ozzie's latest venture in an early August letter: "Quite an honor to fly B-29s, but I will stick to my pea shooter and have more fun." Lewis, like so many young men from the University was in the Army Air Forces. He was training to be a fighter pilot in the Army's newest fighter aircraft, the North American P-51.

By the end of July, Ozzie was located at Clovis Army Airfield in New Mexico. He expected to be there "Until I go overseas..." he said in a July 29 letter to Charles Crossland back at Maine. It was at Clovis that he would meet his crew as the AAF assigned them to him. Together, they would undergo three months of intensive training flying together practicing bombing and gunnery. The sophistication and advanced technology for those days of the B-29 required close teamwork and bonding of the crew.

Meanwhile, that summer, the pace of the fighting in the war increased. While Allied forces bogged down in Italy, substantial progress was made in France. The Russians had gained the upper hand against the Nazis and were pushing them back toward the German heartland. The Eighth Air Force intensified its bombing campaign against German war industries and sought mastery of the skies over northern Europe. In the Pacific, MacArthur's forces landed in New Guinea from the south while the Marines and Army continued its island-hopping campaign from the west. The strategic air bombing campaign against the Japanese homeland from Chinese airfields began in mid-June. But to bring this campaign closer to Japan and within a more feasible range of the B-29 Superfortress, U.S. Marines assaulted Saipan on June 15. The battle on this volcanic island lasted until July 9 with more than 4,000 Americans killed or injured. Few of the 32,000 Japanese defenders survived the fighting. Soon, other strategic islands within the Northern Marianas fell to the Americans.

Once back in New Mexico, Ozzie was able to connect with his friend Earle who was now stationed for bombardier training at Carlsbad. They visited together at the end of July and their correspondence increased. "Earle and I have been corresponding in much greater volume that we ever did before. I suppose our proximity to each other has had a rather psychological effect which tends to cause that," he said in an August 22 letter to Bricker. In the same letter, he said he was also corresponding with Maynard French more frequently as well. "We've all three of us been having some good old chit-chats!" For Ozzie, though, keeping his dreams of theater

Ozzie's Sketch of F.D.R.

alive through contact with Herschel was crucial. "Now all I need is to hear from you now and then...I do hope you won't be too busy this fall, so that I may hear from you fairly often. More now than ever, I'll want to keep in contact with you." Herschel tried to oblige.

The next few months for Ozzie was a time of internal conflict. He squarely looked at the harsh realities of combat preparation while keeping his dream of theater and his place in the arts alive. He hinted at this struggle in an August 22 letter to Bricker. "I've been doing a little sketching with charcoal--very little! I don't have a lot of free time, but once in awhile I like to dip into the arts a little--it does my heart good, somehow. It makes me quite happy and almost free of these bonds the Army has on me!" He continued to dabble in various art forms that fall as time allowed. Yet, he knew that his time in the states was limited as he stated in this same letter, "I expect to ship out and across sometime around the first part of December. Where? I don't know, but I have a general idea, and being in B-29s almost cinches the Theater of Operations as being the Far East! Probably India or China or Saipan or Guam, or possibly Burma." His third guess was correct.

Crew training that late summer and fall went well. Ever personable and friendly, Ozzie, in a fatherly way, cemented the crew together to face the tough job ahead of them. He went out of his way for his men even attending the wedding of his radar man, Howie Coster. Howie's wife Audrey wrote, "He was so nice about our wedding. Mom Coster said that Ozzie was such a nice fellow. He was with her most of the time and she certainly enjoyed knowing him." Milt Smith, Ozzie's young navigator, gave him wedding photos of his marriage to Mary Davenport that summer. The crew responded positively to Ozzie, and their morale was high. "I, too, think the whole crew was fine. Everyone was swell and really took such an interest in his job," wrote Audrey. Ozzie, though, remained troubled. "I fear some of my philosophy at this point would not be, well, too good. At the moment I am pondering over what I've learned about the mess that humanity and civilization really is underneath its beautiful shell," he wrote in an September letter to Bricker. "Some other time, Herschel," he concluded. In earlier letters to Bricker, Ozzie mentioned that he had grown up because of his experience and that this was a quality that would make him a better actor. Now, though, he bordered on disillusionment.

Ozzie was thrilled when Bricker informed him that he would produce *Prelude to Courage* that fall. "Really, it gives me a grand feeling inside to know it might be actually produced somewhere. Sort of makes me feel as if I were still back there in theater--actively. Please, please do it one way or another if you can," Ozzie wrote September 3. Ozzie did not write to Bricker again, and then only briefly, until September 22, nearly three weeks later. "Don't have time for much more," he said. The pace of training had intensified at Clovis and Ozzie was hard pressed to find free time. The anticipated December departure date for the Pacific Theater of Operations (PTO) was rapidly approaching, but he did promise to send Bricker the requested revisions to his play.

Another two weeks passed before Ozzie next wrote to Herschel. His October 5 letter was uncharacteristically brief and rushed. He asked about the progress of producing his play and put in a special request: "I wish if you do it at Maine in the Little Theater, that you'd get in touch with my folks. I know that they'd love to see it. Would you do that for me?" Again, he mentioned dabbling in an art form, this time music.

He told Bricker that he bought a trumpet and a self-instruction book. He admitted, though, that "It's tough on the neighbors."

Ozzie expressed some frustration when Bricker wrote that Ozzie's revisions didn't make much of a difference. "I did feel that the revisions weren't quite as weak as the original even with as little time as I had to put on it!" Ozzie wrote. And in a response uncharacteristic of Ozzie, he berated himself and belittled his play. "And incidentally, when you get right down to it I'm hardly what one could consider an author or playwright anyway, so what can be expected but a piece of work with many weak spots--and lacking in finish etc! Hell 'Prelude' was just something I did to amuse myself about two years ago when I was in the hospital for a week. Frankly I thought it smelled from the beginning." Having vented his frustration, he concluded: "But I'm glad you liked it and I'm getting a real lift out of knowing that it's being presented up there...I'm sure your production of it will be grand and will make the play a big hit."

Herschel told Ozzie he was concerned about Earle, who had recently expressed his growing bitterness. Ozzie was surprised and said he would write to him, but defended his friend: "Perhaps you are a bit naive about understanding service men's problems. I don't think anyone can completely understand another's problems unless he is living under the same circumstances. You must remember that Earle is working under a good deal of pressure--this cadet business is a rugged existence--and he's bound to be on edge and mentally frustrated at times. When I was a cadet, there were times I just felt that I couldn't stand the pressure another moment. The attitude of 'What's the use' nearly took its toll on me a dozen times, and did take its toll on other boys."

Meanwhile, back at the Maine Masque, Ozzie's play was produced in the Little Theater on Tuesday evening, October 31 and Wednesday evening, November 1. Ozzie imagined the scene and expressed his appreciation to Bricker for inviting his folks in a November 5 letter: "I'm glad you remembered to ask them. I'm sure it meant a lot to them to be able to sit there in the Little Theatre where they once came to dote on their boy as he carried on and cut capers before the footlights, and this time to see a play written by him and produced by the same theater group and same grand director! It must have been a most warming sensation they felt as they sat there listening, watching and at the same time reminiscing. My folks, whether they be justified or not, like all parents, are proud of their son in any effort he may make, in any ability or talent he may show, no matter how small it may actually be."

Two days later, Ozzie received a letter from Herschel highlighting the audiences' positive response to *Prelude to Courage*. "You might say I'm walking on clouds tonight!" Ozzie said in his November 7 reply. " I was terribly moved by your letter and the copy of the 'Campus'." The November 2 issue of the *Maine Campus* included a story on the performance and an editorial stating: "We believe that the philosophy contained (in the play) exemplifies a feeling prevalent among the youth of today especially those who are serving in Uncle Sam's armed forces." Ozzie wrote: "It's hard to explain the kind of feeling I have inside me now, but you being a theater person must have put on a fine production...I'm very happy about the whole thing and I feel more than ever that I'm still taking an active part in theater, small as it may be."

The success of the play prompted Herschel to suggest that

Ozzie consider playwriting as a career. Ozzie responded: "You know my real love in theater is the actual business of production, either acting or directing," but he pressed Herschel for his opinion on his career: "Straight from the shoulder, Herschel, do you feel my future is in writing or acting and directing?" Ozzie asked. "If I have something inside me that I should give the world (as you say I do) then I definitely want to do all I can in that direction...I'm looking for facts and 'reading' on the future." News about the success of his play back home made him hopeful and Ozzie ended his November 7 letter: "Well Herschel, I think I feel far happier tonight than I've felt in a long time-thanks to you."

Prelude to Courage was the focus of Ozzie's next letter to Bricker two weeks later. By this time he had heard from his parents. "I think my mother paid the greatest tribute possible to the play, the cast, and you--you in particular," he said on November 15th, quoting his mother: "'Before the lights came up on stage, the organ played very softly...'My Buddy.' It made the chills go up and down your spine. It was so lovely the way that built up the atmosphere. I think during this the house lights dimmed and Steve came on stage...While he (John Emerson Sr.) was speaking it dawned on me slowly that somewhere very faintly and sweetly the organ was playing "Abide With Me". It was so touching and beautiful-- I shall never forget it. You would have loved it and I think you'd have cried at your own little play. Daddy was so wrapped up in the J.E. speech that he didn't remember the musical background. It (the whole thing) shook him up pretty much. The music was so faint that I wonder if it was my imagination.'"

Other Maine performances of Ozzie's one act play soon followed. The Bangor High Drama Club performed it for the

Bangor Quipus, the Athene Club, and the Bangor-Brewer Lions Club. The Maine Masque performed it again at the Dow Field hospital, and the play was performed at the annual convention of the State Teachers' Association in Lewiston. *The Bangor Daily News* ran a feature story in its Saturday-Sunday edition of February 10, 1945 titled: "Young Bangor Aviator Develops Literary Skill; Writes Little Play." The article stated: "What makes this little story distinctive is that Lieut. Keith has not only learned to be a fighter, he has learned to be a writer, too. Or, more accurately, contact with the most dramatic of all stories, the war, has brought out and developed his natural talent." The article implied a bright future in the literary arts for Ozzie:" A great deal of literature has already been born from this war's agony. There will be a great deal more, for many years, after the guns are stilled. And at least some of it has come from young soldiers, previously unknown outside their home communities, who had it in them to write and, in the midst of heroism, suffering, sacrifice, and tragic drama, developed literary self-expression. That is one of America's hopes for the future."

Earle Rankin visited Ozzie from Carlsbad November12. They talked theater. "I really enjoyed Sunday more than any day I've spent in months," Ozzie said. It was a brief interlude from the reality for now of combat preparation. While he hoped for a leave before going overseas, he admitted to Bricker November 15 that the chances were not good: "It seems we're really needed over there now. Keep things going till we all get back," he said. The end of December was rapidly approaching. Earle Rankin reported in an early December letter to Bricker that Ozzie was working on a new play and he hoped they could get together one more time before he shipped out. "Ozzie's tops with me, " Earle said.

Left to right: Leighton Mishou, Wayne Plummer, Charles Neil, J. Palmer Libby.

Bangor High School Drama Club Performing *Prelude to Courage*

At Clovis, crew training neared its completion for Ozzie and his men. Their training was rigorous. Washington established strenuous training standards for bombardment crews. Craven and Cate in their monumental post war Army Air Forces history titled *The Army Air Forces in World War II* describes these: "Crew members were to understand their responsibilities not only for their particular jobs but also to each other; they were to complete successful tests in sustained high-altitude flights, evasion exercises, and precision bombing runs. Units had to demonstrate their ability to take off, assemble, and land together; to operate in the air under radio silence and through overcast; to fly all types of formations; and to execute simulated bombardment missions." Crew training comprised three parts: instruction in individual specialties; combat crew teamwork; and, simulations of actual combat missions. All this training was done within an atmosphere of sharing life together. "The crew was the family circle of an air force; each member knew that long hours of work, play, anxiety, and danger would be shared," Craven and Cate stressed.

While Ozzie had seen a B-29 at Lincoln, he and his crew did not train on one. A severe shortage of the new bombers prevented that. National priority required that these aircraft be immediately deployed to the battle zone. Instead, Ozzie's crew trained on a "war- weary" B-17. Yet, the focus of training remained the B-29. All crew members attended hours of ground school classes on the new and sophisticated war machine. When they went on simulated long flights to Cuba or other Carribean islands, Ozzie and his crew pretended that they were indeed flying the B-29. These day and night simulated combat missions gave each crew member an opportunity to practice his specialty. The bombardier, Bob Broitzman, practiced bombing by dropping sacks of flour on targets; the navigator, Milt Smith, guided the ship to the objective and back to base; the gunners, Dugan, Barry, Flick, and Caruso, practiced their skills by shooting at drones pulled by other aircraft; and the flight engineer, Larry Helmke, practiced monitoring the B-29s complex operating systems. Larry's work allowed Ozzie and his co-pilot James Bunga to focus on the aircraft's direction and altitude. Howie Coster worked the radar while Mickey Seel kept in radio contact with the outside world.

Ozzie and his crew were sent to Kearney Army Air Field in Kearney, Nebraska on December 17. There, they would be processed for dispatching to the Pacific war zone. They would also pick up their B-29, a new aircraft manufactured under Boeing license by Bell Aircraft in Marietta, Georgia.

During a December 10 visit with Earle, Ozzie poured "out his heart" to his Maine Masque friend; Earle passed Ozzie's career misgivings on to Bricker in a December 17 letter. Ozzie expressed his discouragement at returning to Maine after the war for three more years of academic study. He had only completed one full year before he was drafted. Earle stated: "He really isn't getting younger," Earle wrote. "I don't believe he's in the mood for long years (3 or more) of study and training." He noted that, except for some occasional forays into theater while in the Army Air Forces, Ozzie had been away from active involvement in theater for three long years. Then Earle revealed a side of Ozzie seldom seen: "Ozzie's very tired, weary and has a great deal of the indifference or bitterness that is the disease of so many servicemen...At any rate, he, like all of us, often wants only to escape to peace and quiet and a nice, steady, minor job of obscurity. Such a lad won't want years more of school even when he gets back on his feet, out of his rut, and his ambition back."

Earle attributed Ozzie's discouragement to what he called G.I.itis and suggested a possible solution. He encouraged Ozzie to spend a year at Pasadena Playhouse after the war to develop his acting ability. "If you want to do Ozzie a favor, then sell him the idea I'm attempting," Earle said, "that of developing all his own personal talents as quickly and as definitely as possible." If Ozzie were found good enough, then he could quickly move into a professional acting career in Hollywood or Broadway as did many from Pasadena. "He needs the chance to develop greater faith in himself and the possible work of his contributions--in a broader theater world with more purpose behind it than escape," Earle advised Herschel.

Bricker suggested that Ozzie consider a career in nonprofessional and community theater after the war. This career route, as opposed to the professional route of acting and performing, required that Ozzie complete his university studies. Then he could teach or work in community theater. Rankin felt Ozzie looked at non-professional theater "...as a place of peace and quiet and calm, a haven for his weariness, and escape for himself and what he considers his inferior talents because he is afraid, a place where he can contribute without a battle." Ozzie's conundrum, Earle argued, was: "He now lacks the drive and ambition necessary to acquire the academic requirements for college teaching and theater direction. He also lacks the faith in himself to tackle professional theater." Earle begged Bricker to help Ozzie "Get faith, not lead him to mere escapism," by insisting that he complete his college education first. In Earle's mind, Bricker, a constant guiding star for Ozzie, should encourage him to try his hand at acting at Pasadena. If that didn't work out for Ozzie, "Perhaps then he'll develop the desire and ambition to delve as deeply as necessary, academically, to acquire a nice obscure, ivory-towered non-pro theater position, " Earle speculated. "So please aim at showing Ozzie the quickest way to prove to himself his own worth. Once that is done, Ozzie can handle his own problems in theater best himself," Earle pleaded for his friend. "And I guess no matter what life will do to him, he can take care of it now."

Chapter Eight

The Letter

> "If you believe in God and the hereafter, death is beautiful and can be looked forward to rather that dreaded."
>
> Man to Steve in *Prelude to Courage*

By December 22, Ozzie and his crew were at Kearney Army Air Field awaiting orders to leave for the Pacific war zone. They had their new B-29 which they named *The Ghastly Goose*. They were assigned to the 497th Bombardment Group, 73 rd Wing, XXI Bomber Command, XX Air Force which was stationed as Isley Field, Saipan, the Northern Marianas. In a matter of days, they would fly west over half the continental United States and then far over the Pacific Ocean. The last few days at Clovis were rushed as were the first few at Kearney. The crew busied itself in war preparation, but Ozzie had time to write to his mentor, his link to a life after the war.

Ozzie's letter was upbeat. He spoke of visiting Earle at Carlsbad and of talking theater through the night and into the morning. He hated to say good-bye to his friend from his Maine Masque days. Acting with Earle in *Hamlet* that spring in 1941 now seemed like a century ago. So much had happened in the world, and so much had happened to Ozzie since those days. And in that month, the progress of the war seemed stalled. Hitler launched a major offensive against Allied forces through the Ardennes, and allied progress against German forces in Italy bogged down in winter rains, snow, and mud. The Russian advance from the east slowed. In the Pacific, Japanese resistance was as tough as ever, and much blood was shed. War planners in Washington now said the Pacific war would last well into the year 1946. Even Hitler, little heard from for several weeks, predicted Germany would fight into 1946!

Any hope Ozzie had of getting home for Christmas to see his family was out of the question. "Leaves are a thing of the past for me until I've served my tour of duty overseas...," he said. It would be his third Christmas away from home. But it was wartime, and Ozzie wanted to "...get across and get into the thing!...I don't want to tell my grandchildren someday that I fought the battle of New Mexico when they ask me what I did in the great war!...I'm anxious to go get the job done," he wrote to Herschel. "I couldn't have a better opportunity than I have now to do a real job for myself, for my country, for humanity. My crew is 'tops', my plane is 'tops'and there is no reason in the world why we shouldn't go through this mess and come back without a scratch, all in one piece."

In this letter, Ozzie exuded the positivism and optimism that so characterized his letters to Bricker over the three years since he left for war. The discouragement that Earle Rankin had written to Bricker about earlier in the month had seemed to dissipate. In fact, Ozzie was working on a new play. Delving once more into theater allowed him "... to get away from realism for a while." He enthusiastically described his new play, still untitled, to his mentor: " In my mind or should I say, my heart, I feel that this play has something...that I feel inside me." His protagonist is an injured soldier, just returned from the war, who, in 1941, was an aspiring and successful artist. After the war his paintings lack what Ozzie calls " the touch." His injury keeps him from holding a normal job and his pension won't sustain him and his wife. A couple of war buddies visit them and talk about what they went

I
OFFICERS' LOUNGE
Army Air Field
Clovis, New Mexico

Curtain rises —

Shabby but neat room — old iron bed left stage — door backstage center window to its right - cheap curtains — door stage left — few pictures on wall — gas 3 burner stove on small table at foot of bed downstage — coffee pot & other utensils table — center stage with lamp — books etc! In corner between center door & right wall — artists equipment — canvasses etc — some complete — some half complete — some bare —

Betty is a small girl — a bit on the pale side — about 24 — not pretty — could be attractive with the right clothes — hair do etc — she's dressed in a rather cheap housedress — her hair neat but rather poor in appearance — stands beside the window gazing out into the street — after a moment she idly crosses the room towards the table — but before she reaches the table — she sees the paintings in the corner upstage right and changes her course to go to them — she goes to her knees — beside them and taking the first one — she picks it up — holds it off

Script of Unfinished Play

through together. This recollection inspires him to paint a picture of a battle in the south Pacific. Through painting he realizes that what is missing from his artwork is, as Ozzie describes it, "Heart-feeling! "And the thing that killed that heart and feeling was of course the hell of war that he had gone through, and like amnesia, the recalling of it brought back the heart-- the feeling--and he once again turns out some fine paintings." Throughout his new play, Ozzie wanted to set the mood as, "... the warmth of love. The little things that make love what it is are woven all through the plot." His new play would be successful if the audience left the theater with "...a warm glowing feeling in their hearts, a feeling of the glory of love and life. Only then will I feel that I have written the play the way I wanted to."

Ozzie spent Christmas that year with his wartime friend, 1st Lt. Francis H. Roth Jr. ("Franny") at his home in Hastings, Nebraska, not far from Kearney where he and his crew were stationed. Franny recalled that Ozzie, "Was so full of the seasonal spirit..." that Christmas. Then, Franny took his friend over to Kearney and despite the extreme cold, "...his presence lent a warmth that was always there when Ozzie was around." Ozzie and Franny had become friends when they were both posted to Carlsbad and then to Hobbs. And Franny had some theatrical experience which bonded these friends even more. "As we shook hands in a last farewell," Franny recalled, " Ozzie said we would meet in Bangor when the mess was over...he was looking into the future."

Earle Rankin was less optimistic about the future prospects for his friend. "He'll be in the Saipan soup soon. God, why must many harmless, innocent, good, clean lads have to suffer the tortures and infamy of the damned before they can reach the calm of death?" Earle mused in a letter to Bricker,

"I hated to see Ozzie go so bad. I'll be glad to go and join him." This absence or longing perhaps drove Earle's somewhat dire and theatrical prognostications for Ozzie's future.

The Ghastly Goose left Kearney on Wednesday, January 3, 1945 and headed west over the Rocky Mountains. The crew was ready; Ozzie was ready. Late that day, they landed at Mather Army Air Field where they would stay for a few days before flying the first leg of their island hopping flight over the Pacific Ocean to Oahu, a distance of approximately 2,500 miles. While at Mather, Ozzie and his crew went through the last checks they would have while stateside. This included filling out a last will and testament. Ozzie's will, dated January 4, left everything to his father, Edgar. The flight out of Kearney gave the crew an opportunity to become familiar with the B-29, which was not available for their training at Clovis as B-29s could not be spared for instruction. They liked their new aircraft and as time went on, became comfortable with it. The B-29 represented the greatest technological and industrial achievement of the American wartime economy.

By January 8, Ozzie and crew were in Hawaii. He told Bricker simply that he was somewhere on Oahu. "B-29 crews are confined to the base here because of their classification as Super-Secret! So I haven't seen anything of the Island except from the air. It's might pretty from what I have seen." His letter was brief, and he predicted that his letters "...Are going to be mighty short for awhile."

It was a long trip hopping across the Pacific Ocean. Yet flying from one island to another was the only way to get the massive gas-hungry bomber to where it was needed. At each island, the aircraft was gassed-up and serviced; the crew rested. After leaving Oahu, Ozzie flew the B-29 to Johnston Island, a tiny atoll in the middle of the Pacific. Milt Smith, his navigator, did an outstanding job keeping the massive bomber on course and on time. From Johnston, they flew to Kwajalein Island. One year before, American forces wrested control of the island from the Japanese, a struggle which proved to be a costly fight. Ozzie then flew the B-29 the last leg into Saipan, one of several contiguous islands freed from Japanese control since the past summer. Indeed, some Japanese soldiers were still in Saipan's remote hills. Finally, *The Ghastly Goose* touched down at Isley Field, Saipan, Northern Marianas on Sunday, January 14. This was the Pacific Theater of Operation (PTO) ; this was the war zone.

"Well, I'm more or less settled now, Ozzie wrote to Bricker the day after he and his crew arrived. "After living out of a tiny duffel bag for about two weeks it sure feels good to have some permanent place to spread things out and have some things to use and know where you can get at it!" He could not say where he was (" Ah well, that's censorship for you."), but he liked the warm days and cool nights and was happy that the island had few mosquitoes--none infected with malaria. "I'm happy Herschel! As you know, I've wanted combat for a long time and now I'm in the thick of it! It looks like a long hard grind, but when I come back, I'll feel much better about having been to combat." He looked forward to his first combat mission, and promised to write Herschel about it as soon as possible.

Since the fall of 1944, Ozzie signed his letters to Bricker with the term "Affectionately." Herschel Bricker wrote to his Maine Masquers serving in the military in a fatherly way, often offering paternal advice. And over the course of the war, Ozzie and Herschel had grown close. Indeed, Ozzie wrote

Herschel January 23, 1944, "...it's good to hear you say you're behind me ("no matter what")! Somehow there's something very substantial in the knowledge of that! You're nowhere near old enough to be my father, of course, but I was rather flattered at the relationship inferred anyhow! As a matter of fact, if I didn't have such a swell dad, I can think of nobody I'd rather have for a father than your honorable self!" And now more than ever and more than half-way around the globe, Ozzie needed the support of people he loved and admired.

Ozzie also wrote to Charles Crossland, Executive Secretary of the University of Maine Alumni Association, updating his address. He indicated he was uncertain as to how long his tour of duty would be but said he was looking forward to returning. "So keep things running for me and all the other boys who still 'stand and drink a toast once again' to the college of our hearts always." Crossland responded with congratulations on his play that had been produced twice recently in Bangor.

By the first part of February, Ozzie and his crew still had not been on a mission. Ozzie was not happy. "I'm still alive and kicking! And you may take *that* literally," he wrote to Bricker. "I'm kicking day in and day out about the set up in general around here. I still haven't been on a raid, and the monotony of sitting around here is just beginning to get on my nerves." His litany of discontent continued in laments that he could not become settled enough even to work on his new play: "The atmosphere over here is not exactly conducive to creative writing of any sort! It seems ages since I last had any contact with theater at all. Lord but I'll be glad when I can once more have nothing to worry about but the little problems of the dramatic arts." He begged Herschel to "Write

Austin's Army Air Force Photograph

soon." For Ozzie, Bricker represented a post-war life in theater; it was his ultimate dream. Herschel was also a connection to a time when Ozzie had found himself, after a period of drift, through acting in a variety of sophisticated roles. And that time, though brief, was a magical moment.

Still, Ozzie's inner awareness of his own mortality belied his outward confidence. He had a feeling about himself that he could not explain, and he had many doubts about his future. Even though he was keenly aware that with combat came the possibility of death, and the end of all earthly endeavors, he yearned to act on a major stage, put his vivid imagination to life through drama, and contribute to American theater. For more than two years, he had wrestled with this conflict that could paralyze his ability to perform his function as an officer. He was experiencing the very essence of his play, *Prelude to Courage*. Faith in God gave him the strength to go on and to realize the courage he needed to face combat.

It was not uncommon for a WWII serviceman facing combat to write a "last" letter to loved ones. The serviceman then gave the letter to a trusted friend to mail should something happen to him. John Ciardi in his diary *Saipan* talks about this very thing. Upon hearing that the new general LeMay wanted to lower the bombing altitudes over Japan, Ciardi, who was a gunner with the 500 Bombardment Group, said: " That was the night I sat down and wrote a letter home to be mailed in case I didn't come back."

Ozzie did likewise. Since childhood days, Ozzie had a keen sense of the future, and now he wanted to share his feelings with his closest loved ones, his parents. Ozzie wrote a letter to them on Sunday, January 28, 1945 -- a letter that is both surreal and elegiac but which masterfully revealed his greatest fear:

Dear Mother and Dad,

I hope this letter may never reach you; because, like most normal people, I want very much to go on living in this old world a little longer. The fact is, if this letter does reach you, I won't any longer be of this world. I'm writing to you tonight, because I have a strange feeling that my days are numbered. Perhaps, my foreboding is completely a figment of my imagination. I hope so, but I wanted you to know a little of what I feel tonight.

This is the first time I've ever felt this close to death. It's a strange feeling--sitting here calmly and thinking that perhaps in a matter of days, all my plans, all my dreams, all my little but so important endeavors will possibly be but memories to those I love and leave behind me. Like shadows that fade when darkness comes--like veils that are but mist and dissipate when the Almighty pours the sun's rays upon the world; like these my successes, failures, hopes, and dreams, will fade and dissipate from view but will be always remembered by my family and friends. The shadow and the mist, once seen, are not forgotten, even when they're no longer visible to the eye. Would that I might have the opportunity to realize my dreams, to test my possibilities, to try my plans, to see my hopes materialize, or even to fail miserably in all this--but to live, and try, and know one way or the other. Now I may never know!

Sitting here, facing the vast unknown in the world beyond, facing the uncertainties of what lies ahead in the hereafter, it's terribly hard to stick to my convictions--to stand by my philosophy of the fear of death. It's really all theory, and when the moment comes that you are actually in the position that you've often philosophized about, it's quite different. Frankly, my heart is full of fears; and to know that everything happens for the best is really <u>little</u> in the way of comfort. In my soul, of course, I know that God's judgment is never to be questioned, so if He wills that I shall die, then so be it!

Then there is the matter of whether or not I deserve recognition in the Kingdom of Heaven. I'm not immune to sin, and thus am not exempt from the possibility of spending the unknown future in hell, even though I may not be one of God's incorrigibles. It's funny how strong the belief in God and his doctrines can suddenly become, when one faces a crisis--especially a crisis dealing with death. He's pulled me through some mighty tight spots, and, now in the <u>tightest,</u> I only wish I might have appreciated, even more, His answering of my prayers in my other crises. Oh, I was most thankful at the time of each crisis--most humble and appreciative. But the periods of time between each crisis--during those, I fear my worship of Him was far from up to the standards of a good Christian. I said my prayers--I believed in Him and his teachings, but I came no where near to living up to his commandments, for I am but another weak mortal man. My worship of Him was devout, but intermittent. And if I should live on for many years yet, I doubt that my brand of worship and Christianity would be any different. I base this doubt on past performances only, because at the moment I am in the throes of another crisis--and at these times I am always want to reach out to God for His aid and comfort, a great deal more than at other times.

Up to now, my prayers to Him have been to the effect that I hoped he'd do everything for the best, and I prayed that whatever his judgment might be--I believed in Him enough so that I would never doubt the feasibility of His acts, and to do with me what he would. Now I find it hard to not ask safety for myself--to not ask Him to see me through this and bring me safely home. I find it difficult to say to Him " Dear God--give me the strength and the will, to be brave in the hours of danger, in the presence of death, and to know that if this be the day for me to die, then that is Thy will, and that Thou hast planned it thus for a reason--even though it may be beyond my power of understanding. And should you see fit to lift my soul from my body, may it be worthy of recognition in Heaven, and may my Faith in Thee never falter, even for a moment, as my love for thee never shall."

I find it difficult, because I'm afraid of the possibility of dieing soon and want more than anything to pray for my life. But--deep down--I believe that prayer-- and pray that way--I do, even though my heart is always filled with the fear of death being close at hand.

And so dear Dad and Mother, you know now a little something of how I feel as I face the possibility of never seeing any of you again. You can also imagine how a man must feel when he actually faces death and <u>knows</u> he's going to die--whereas mine is only a premonition.

I want you to know that I have had the best life anyone could ever dare hope for, and the reason for it is that I have had the two grandest parents in the world. And that goes for the rest of the family. I love you all as much as it is possible to love anyone. And I only wish I might have come home to be with you all again.

As I told you at the beginning--this letter will never reach you unless something happens to me. So--if you receive this dear family--I'll be somewhere in the great beyond--and this will be something like a word from beyond the grave.

And now that I've had this little talk with you, in which I feel God was sitting with us, I feel much better--my mind is settled and I feel a sort of peaceful comfort within me that I haven't known for a long while.

And so goodnight until we may be together again in the promised land.

                    Your loving son,

                    Austin.

Chapter Nine

Abide With Me, Fast Falls the Eventide

> "I began to feel all over again that there's just too much water in the Pacific. It's a sort of gaudy extravagance."
>
> John Ciardi, *Saipan*

Ponderous Peg continued its northwestward trek toward Japan. Ozzie enjoyed his break from flying the powerful B-29 and his reminiscences, but now it was time to take back flying the mammoth bomber from Lt. Katchmir, his co-pilot. Ozzie had sought combat since graduating from Advanced Flight Training in December, 1942. Today, February 25, 1945, more than two years later, Ozzie was leading his crew in its fourth mission. Their target was Tokyo.

Milt Smith called Ozzie over the aircraft's interphone. He told the airplane commander that they were approaching the wing assembly area just west of the Bonin Islands and should be at the rendezvous point in approximately 15 minutes. They had made good time flying nearly 800 miles at 250 mph; now they were more than half way to Tokyo. Ozzie acknowledged Milt's message and noted that off to the left of Ponderous Peg over the horizon lay Iwo Jima which was currently under siege by American marines. That island's capture from the Japanese would eliminate enemy radar and radio stations and provide a base for American fighter aircraft. The island was one more step in the relentless move of the American military forces closer to Japan's heartland. Both officers knew that it would provide a safe landing strip for damaged B-29s on their way back from bombing missions.

Too many bombers were now being lost at sea. He thought briefly of the crew's original B-29, The Ghastly Goose, which they had flown together to the war zone six weeks ago. The Ghastly Goose was lost on January 27th when Lt. Peterson was forced to land in the ocean off Japan after sustaining battle damage during a bombing mission over Tokyo. But Iwo Jima wouldn't help Ozzie and his crew today should they need it.

As Ozzie took back control of Ponderous Peg from Wassil, he needed every bit of concentration he could muster for the mission ahead. Wassil noted some turbulence and strong winds. Ozzie agreed as he had felt the massive aircraft occasionally shudder and vibrate during his time of reflection, but soon they would begin to climb to the bombing altitude where the winds may be calmer. Once they arrived at the wing assembly area, it would take Ponderous Peg and the other aircraft in the squadron more than 30 minutes to climb to bombing altitude. From there, they would form a tight formation for protection as they approached the Japanese mainland. Together, he and Wassil would need to keep Ponderous Peg headed in the proper direction and at the correct altitude.

On the tail surface of each B-29, the Army Air Forces numbered the aircraft under the bombardment group's alpha logo. Ponderous Peg was number A-44 of the 871st squadron. Flying to Ozzie's rear was number A-45 of the same squadron piloted by 1st Lieutenant Jack S. Barnes. Off to Ozzie's right side was number A-51 also of the 871st squadron flown by 1st Lieutenant Robert J. Anderson. From Saipan, the aircraft had flown in single file well apart from each other. As they approached the wing assembly area, they would come closer together and form a protective echelon crucial to formation flying. The pilots occasionally communicated with each other over the aircraft's VHF command radio, but they were under strict orders from headquarters to use the radio only when necessary. The Japanese were listening.

Ozzie liked formation flying. As an air cadet, he had to master this skill. He also helped new air cadets master the technique when he was a flight instructor with the Army Air Forces Training Command. Formation flying took tremendous skill and attention; everything pilots had learned and had practiced would be tested. Also, formation flying during the bombing run produced better bombing results; headquarters and Washington were looking for that.

A few minutes remained before reaching the wing assembly point giving Ozzie an opportunity to check in with each crew member. Most likely, they too were wondering about the next few hours and what challenges they would face. The Japanese defenders always seemed to be full of surprises. No mission was a repetition of a previous mission; something unexpected always happened. Since the crew's arrival in Saipan, they had heard stories about the experiences of other crews in combat. Yet, Ozzie would reassure each one with his confidence. Just two days ago, he wrote to his friend Earle and described the missions they had been on so far: "We've been lucky to date--never a scratch to crew or plane..."

Ozzie tried to convey a sense of pride within his crew about the importance of their mission and to engender within them an eagerness to carry it out. So when he called each one, he was cheery and reassuring. He first called Flight Officer Broitzman who had just returned to his station in the glassed-in nose of the aircraft and who was making some last minute adjustments to the Norden Bomb Sight. He had been visiting Mickey Seel in the radio area of the front compartment of the aircraft. There, they were talking about music, something they both loved. Bob was fine. Ozzie then called Larry, the flight engineer. His back faced forward and they joked about how he could see where they had been but not where they were going. Larry also had a small window to look out on the right wing so he could see how the two engines there each with a sixteen foot propeller were performing. Behind Larry, sat Mickey who was busy with the radios monitoring command channels. He told Ozzie when called that everything was working well with no noticeable interference. Milt, always busy, continued to plot the course to Japan, but he told Ozzie when asked that they were on target. Next, he called his gunners in the mid-section of the aircraft beyond the bomb bays. Charlie Dugan and Bob Flick assured their captain that their eyes were already pealed for Japanese fighters. Gene Barry was also scanning the skies and told Ozzie that they were ready for a fight. Howie Coster was adjusting his radar set when Ozzie called him in his windowless compartment. While the weather outside was beautiful, this could change rapidly as they approached Japan. Indeed, the weather forecast indicated that it was overcast over Tokyo. Most likely they would need to use the radar today to bomb. Consequently, Howie would have to work closely with Flight Officer Broitzman. Howie again thanked Ozzie for coming to his wedding. The airplane commander then called the last man on his crew, Luigi. He told his skipper that he was ready to give it to the Japanese and not to worry about him. They joked about him being at the end of the aircraft--the last but certainly not the least. While exuding reassurance, Ozzie still worried about everyone on his crew.

To Ozzie's right sat his new co-pilot, Wassil. Ozzie didn't know too much about him, but he liked him. He handled the airplane competently when Ozzie rested. Now the B-29 was back in Ozzie's control. Soon Ponderous Peg would be the lead plane in the three plane v-shaped echelon. He looked out over the vast Pacific Ocean below him which seemed to go on endlessly. "I began to feel all over again that there's just too much water in the Pacific. It's a sort of gaudy extravagance." Lt. Barnes was coming up from the rear to get into his place on the left and to the rear of the formation. Lt. Anderson was still off to the right. He would join the echelon once Barnes in A-45 was in place. It was 10:46 am. Suddenly, Luigi screamed into the interphone: "Skipper watch out!" Ozzie saw, then knew.

Horrifying noise -- blinding light -- engulfing flame -- searing heat ... then silence...

> Abide with me, fast falls the eventide;
> The darkness deepens, Lord with me abide;
> When other helpers fail and comforts flee,
> Help of the helpless, O abide with me...

"This is the first time I've ever felt this close to death...."
The Results of the Mid-air Collision

Chapter Ten

At 10 Boynton Street:
Cum Magno Me Delore

"Is *this* what became of us?"

Johnny in *Jim Dandy*
played by Austin Rodney Keith
The Maine Masque Theatre, December 17, 18, 1941
The University of Maine

For Edgar Keith, Friday, March 2, 1945 began like any other day. He picked up the Bangor Daily News off his front porch and quickly scanned the front page. It was full of war news. It seemed as if Allied forces were making significant progress against the Axis powers. "MacArthur's Men Land On Palawan..." one headline read. American forces seized control of the largest Philippine island from Japanese forces, the article said. In Europe, Patton's men were moving into the German city of Cologne. As he paged through the rest of the newspaper, he found a composite picture, titled "The Spirit of '76 Marches On" on page 11. The New York Sun had taken Joe Rosenthal's famous picture of American marines raising the Stars and Stripes atop Mount Suribachi, Iwo Jima, and placed Archibald Williard's famous painting, "The Spirit of '76" to the upper right of Rosenthal's photograph. This composite photograph effectively linked past American history to the costly American sacrifice necessary to the capturing of Iwo Jima, now nearly complete. Indeed, two days later, the first B-29 in trouble after bombing Japan would land there; more than 2,000 other bombers over the remaining months of the war would follow suit.

What really struck Edgar that morning as he looked at the newspaper was a front page picture of B-29s in a bombing run on a Japanese supply depot in Rangoon, Burma. Of course he thought of Austin and wondered how he was. Ozzie was a faithful letter writer, but they hadn't had a letter for a few days. Edgar assumed that Ozzie was pretty busy these days now that he and his crew were actively involved in bombing Japan.

Before Edgar headed off to work, he needed to brush off his 1940 Oldsmobile as it had snowed the night before. The early morning sun was peaking through clouds over Bangor, and the forecast predicted a sunny day with temperatures in the mid-30s. It had been a long winter with a lot of snow. Huge icicles hung from the south side of the house and Boynton Street was pretty narrow with the snow piled high on both sides of the street. A few miles to the west, Dow Field had stayed open this winter, unlike other winters since opening. More and more bombers and crews were passing through on their way to Europe as the American war effort intensified.

Bertha kissed Edgar as he headed out to open his appliance store on Park Street. Later he would check on his bowling alley, The Bowlaway, on York Street. Pearl, Bertha's sister who lived with them, would join Edgar at the store in the early afternoon and get caught up on some bookkeeping.

At 12:44 pm, a telegraph was received at the Western Union office on Central Street in Bangor. It needed to be delivered to 10 Boynton Street without delay. Shortly after 1 pm, Bertha heard knocking on the front door. When she peered through the glass and saw who was there, her worst fears rose within her. Could this telegram be about Ozzie? Perhaps, it could be something else. She signed for the telegram, and opened it apprehensively. It simply read:

> M. EDGAR N KEITH
> 10 BOYNTON ST BNGR=
>
> =THE SECRETARY OF WAR DESIRES ME TO EXPRESS HIS DEEP REGRET THAT YOUR SON FIRST LIEUTENANT AUSTIN R. KEITH WAS KILLED IN ACTION ON TWENTY SIX FEBRUARY IN PACIFIC OCEAN AREA CONFIRMING LETTER FOLLOWS=
>
> =A ULIO THE ADJUTANT GENERAL.

Bertha dropped to her knees. Pearl ran over to her sister. She too was horrified when she read the contents of the telegram. Pearl desperately phoned Edgar and told him to come home immediately. Edgar soon arrived and bounded up the front stairs and into the house.

That afternoon was one of chaos within the Keith home. Within an hour after receiving the telegram, the mailman arrived. A letter from Ozzie was part of that day's mail. Ozzie's sister Marion, who was a senior at Bangor High School, arrived home from school and saw her distressed parents. Rev. Arlan A. Bailee, Pastor of All Souls Congregational Church, arrived and stayed well into the evening to provide comfort and solace. Bertha composed herself enough to call Jane Wooster's mother to ask if Jane, Marion's girlhood friend, could come over and be with Marion that night. Jane described that day for the Keiths as, "Awful...They never recovered from this." What followed were years of grief and sorrow: "Cum Magno Me Dolore-to my great sorrow."

Coincidentally, Herschel Bricker was delivering a lecture on current New York theater productions at the Bangor Public Library less than a mile away from 10 Boynton Street that Friday afternoon. In this lecture, Bricker foresaw new drama emerging from the wartime experiences of young men now engaged in combat: "It is they who are carrying the torch; who have thoughts and are not hesitant about expressing them. Some speak the language of the theater. A few may have it in them to speak it eloquently." No doubt he was thinking of Austin with his play *Prelude to Courage* and his new play still unfinished. Soon he would learn the news the Keiths had received. The next day, the Keiths received a letter from Bricker:

> "The news of Austin's death came as a terrible shock. One tries to steel oneself to the possibility of such news, but I guess one can never be prepared. I am sure that you know my sympathy is genuine, because I too came to love him and to have much hope for his future."

> "It is hard to understand why a boy such as Austin is taken from this world; but there is in God's will a reason. Austin was a deeply religious boy in the finest sense, because he lived as he believed. He was truly a great boy--with a heart full of sensitivity, of emotion, of love,--and, I think, of joy in living. He knew how to live--he was self-sufficient. His dabbling--as he called it--with the paints, with clay, and with writing certainly must have given him many hours of genuine satisfaction and happiness."

> "As I write to one of Austin's closest friends, Earle Rankin, I should like to say to you--To have known

Austin has made my life a little fuller and richer; and in my heart there is a desire now to work a little harder for the finer things theater represents--for Austin and for all of 'my' boys who will no longer be working in theater."

One month later, Bricker expressed his sorrow and regret over Austin's death when he spoke to the Women's Literary Union in Auburn where he was interviewed by Marion Cooper, Journal Magazine Editor of the Lewiston Daily Sun. In an April 21 story, the Lewiston Journal reported that: "Prof. Bricker speaks with especial regret of the lost talents of Lt. Austin Keith of Bangor who was killed in an air battle over Tokyo. *'Prelude to Courage,'* an one act play that was almost prophetic in its theme, won a recent one act play contest and showed promise of the fine things the young man might have accomplished had his life been spared."

An announcement about Austin's death and brief obituary appeared in the weekend edition of the Bangor Daily News March 3. Soon tributes came to the Keiths. Bertha kept a log of letters, cards, phone calls, flowers and food the family received, some of which were from family of Ozzie's crew members. During the next year, she made over 200 entries and sent a thank you note for each expression of kindness.

Many moving letters noted Austin's strength of character. His boyhood friend, Charles Bartlett Jr., wrote in the present tense, describing Ozzie as, "...my best friend and always will be--we are far closer than friends--closer even than many twin brothers. There will always be deep rooted feeling...." Bartlett said Ozzie had "...an exceptionally active mind with a vivid imagination. His were all the ideas whenever we did something...."Ozzie's childhood friend credited him with making him a better person: "Ozzie truly had a gift of drawing out the highest qualities in one's character and literally pulling them up to his height, his level...Yes, we were inseparable. Ozzie had that gifted character and leadership that one finds once in a lifetime and when it has gone, the whole world has lost a friend, a helping hand."

A newer friend from the Army Air Forces, Francis H. Roth Jr. wrote, "I have lost a brother. Yes, to me Ozzie was just that. Every boy has a model he wants to follow and imitate. Ozzie was and is mine. I'm not going to think of him as gone for to me he lives now even more than in life itself...We had several personal talks but never once did he show any fear. Ozzie was well prepared. No matter what...."

Bricker got the news out about Austin's death in his letters to former students and in his March 1945 newsletter to Maine Masquers now serving in the military around the world. Some wrote to the Keiths. Weber Mason wrote from Halle, Germany: "Austin and I were classmates at Maine, and my fondest memories are with him and the lovely times we had in connection with the Masque...I am proud that Austin was a member of that group; and, believe me, his winning smile, his wonderful personality will never be forgotten by any of us...We have all suffered a great loss."

Maynard French, a Maine Masquer who visited with Ozzie during the war, wrote to the Keiths, and in a letter to Bricker he wrote: "This is the closest that the war has touched me...You know how much I thought of him and how he was beginning to fit so perfectly into the plans that Earle and I made so long ago for our future in the theater. I shall miss him terribly; he was one in a million. God, Herschel, how many more must go that way before this horrible mess is over!!" Bill Brown, another Masquer, and fraternity brother of Ozzie, wrote Bricker from Germany: "News of Ozzie's death was almost a little more than I could comprehend. Everything seemed so perfect for him...He was a great guy...My only hope is that we can make it up to all the great guys just the way they wanted it done."

Norman Mennes, whom Bricker had brought east from California in 1941 to help in set design for the theater program and who visited Ozzie during the war, wrote this poem as a tribute:

> These cannot speak; their tongues are dumb
> They lived, and they have died like men.
> When future generations come
> To view their resting places, then
> They will remember what it cost
> To rescue what was almost lost--
> Freedom, and kindliness, and love,
> Honour, and chivalry most true,
> And all that lifts our hearts above
> Earth's sordid treasures. Comrades, you
> Gave what we might have given,
> Strove where we might have striven,
> And what we offered and willed to give
> You gave. And though you died you live.
> While freedom lasts and men remain
> You have not paid the price in vain

Tributes also came from the University of Maine. *The Maine Campus* student newspaper expressed "...a sincere feeling of sorrow on learning of the death of Lt. Austin Keith." "I feel a sense of real loss," wrote Manning Hawthorne. "I was his English instructor at Maine and saw quite a bit of him...He was one of those students who stand out in a teacher's memory from the crowd of faces that people his years of teaching, and I shall always remember him...I like to think of him as forever young--he will never know the disillusionments, the pain, the trouble of advancing years, and his unquenchable spirit will remain forever free and idealistic and full of the zeal and enthusiasm he had in life. You can always remember him as he is now--a man because of the responsibilities he has faced, but a boy in all the fine ways."

University of Maine President Arthur Hauck wrote to Ozzie's parents: "Austin won a high place in the esteem and affection of everyone who knew him here. In every way he measured up to our ideals for American youth. We were proud to claim him as a student, proud of the willing and courageous service he gave to his country. I hope that you will find comfort in the realization that when he fell he was doing what he wanted to do, playing a man's part in this struggle to preserve the ideals of freedom and justice. The world will be a better place because of the inspiration of his life and sacrifice. As long as there is a University of Maine, the name and memory of Lieutenant Austin R. Keith will be remembered and cherished on this Campus."

Bricker encouraged his "boys" who knew Ozzie to write to the Keiths. Earle Rankin, perhaps Ozzie's closest friend and confidant, could not. "Write and console Ozzie's folks? I wish with all my heart I could," he wrote to Bricker. "What can I say? Your news of Ozzie came this noon--I am still limp and my hand shakes as I write. I cannot find words to really express my bitterness--it's awfully deep and an all-over feeling. It leaves no room for comfort, or faith, or much of anything of aid in times like this. I'm simply helpless, have long been so... Ozzie's death is no more than I sincerely expected deep within me...When I last saw him in Carlsbad and he took the bus back to Clovis--I was sure it was the last time I'd see him. That's why I took pains to stop at Clovis when I got my leave--I knew his days were numbered."

"Wherever his twisted mangled, charred body is, there is a ring on his right hand--I gave it to him in November one late night when we were having a session...Ozzie didn't meet up with anything over there <u>he</u> didn't expect...and (he) went down without a squeak or complaint...he went whole-hog, completely and quickly, none of this half a man left to die a living hell of years. His attitude and philosophy was much the same as mine...he and I thought and felt alike about the war, combat, the Air Forces, theater, etc....He was just as bitter and desperate as I am ...." Unlike what Bricker thought, Earle explained, Ozzie's, "...real philosophy and attitude was far different--what he told you was the usual thing all of us write for civilian consumption."

What made the difference for Ozzie in Earle's mind was his faith. He wrote to Bricker, "I admired him and his courage in facing what all of us must and as he said, 'the uncertainty that only a moron doesn't fear'...He had faith. That faith enabled him to face it and he inspired me and gave me the courage to do the same. Yes, Ozzie had faith--a fine, sincere abounding faith that kept him going and buoyed him up in as deep and dark a despair as mine. Perhaps his bitterness was deeper, for he was even more sensitive than I. I admired Ozzie for his faith--something I lack."

Just two days before he was killed, Ozzie wrote to Earle trying to reassure him, in a sanguine but realistic tone, about the perils of combat: "So you're on you way to combat, buddy. Well need I say I'm sorry? You know how you felt about me going--well--I feel the same way about you and now that I've had three missions and know all the dangers and the percentage of a man coming back--well-I'm more sorry than ever. Don't let that statement startle you. It may not be as bad as it sounds--in fact it probably isn't--but having been subjected to the rawness of it all now, my outlook is somewhat on the grim side. Forgive me for being an alarmist---We've been lucky to date--never a scratch to crew or plane. Pray it will go on." Then, as if he knew his time was near, Ozzie bade his friend farewell: "Thank you, Earle, for being such a grand guy and a wonderful friend."

The Keiths knew little of the circumstances surrounding the death of their beloved son. A March 13 letter from a Major E. A. Bradunas at Headquarters, Army Air Forces in Washington gave the Keiths, in official parlance, the first details of Ozzie's death: "A report has been received in this headquarters concerning the death of your son which states that he was killed in action on February 26, 1945, when the B-29 (Superfortress) bomber of which he was a crew member, collided with another of our aircraft while assembling to participate in a combat mission to Tokyo, Japan. Both aircraft crashed into the sea, and there were no survivors from either plane." A list of the names of the crew members and the addresses of family was included.

Edgar received another official letter, dated March 14, from Lt. Colonel Frank L. Davis, Commander of the 871st Bombardment Squadron in Saipan offering more details surrounding the circumstances of Ozzie's death: "On the morning of the 25th of February this year, Lieutenant Keith, as pilot of a B-29 airplane, participated with his crew in a bombing strike against industrial targets in the Tokyo area. They reached the assembly point. This is the area where the aircraft assume the formation they are to fly over the target. In maneuvering for position your son's ship and another collided. Both ships were severely damaged and plunged into the ocean. Another aircraft from this organization piloted by Lieutenant Robert J. Anderson witnessed the collision and immediately went down low searching for survivors. Several hours were spent by this search crew in thoroughly sweeping the area. Although a few empty life rafts were seen floating away, no survivors were seen."

Further in his letter, Col. Davis spoke about Austin: "Since his arrival here he has always displayed a fierce pride in his mission and an eagerness to carry it out. Truly his accomplishments have been a significant factor in this organization's contribution to the destruction of important military and industrial targets in the heart of the Japanese homeland. His attitude at all times has been the highest example as a gentleman and combat officer. Devotion to duty seemed second nature to him. We all can do well to attempt to meet the standards he attained. We, who fought with him, are proud and inspired in carrying his torch forward with us."

Colonel Davis closed his letter with, "In his sacrifice his efforts were for the protection and happiness of his country and those he loved. I join you in the feeling of assurance that he is happy in the knowledge of an earthly service well done."

Among other official communications, The Chief of Staff, General George C. Marshall sent the Keiths a card that read: "General Marshall extends his deep sympathy in your bereavement. Your son fought valiantly in a supreme hour of his country's need. His memory will live in the grateful heart of our nation." Meanwhile, in a March 27 letter, Major General J. A. Ulio, who had sent the initial telegram informing them of Ozzie's death, officially corrected the date of Ozzie's death to February 25.

In early April, Lieutenant General Barney M. Giles, Chief of Air Staff wrote to the Keiths for General H. H. Arnold, Commanding General, Army Air Forces: "The military reputation of Lieutenant Keith has been called to my attention and I find that he was a most competent officer. He established a fine reputation at Luke Field, and earned the admiration of associates by his conscientious endeavor and devotion to duty. He will be remembered as a pilot of patriotism and courage, and his untimely passing is mourned by all who knew him."

Henry L. Stimson, Secretary of War, sent an April 3 letter to Edgar and informed him that Ozzie, "Who sacrificed his life in defense of his country...," was awarded the Purple Heart. In his letter, the Secretary expressed hope "That time and the victory of our cause will finally lighten the burden of your grief." General Henry H. Arnold, Commanding General of the Army Air Forces, also acknowledged Ozzie's sacrifice in a Memorial Day message: "We are again mindful on this Memorial Day of our debt to those of the Army Air Forces who have given their lives for our country. Their memory is always with us." This message ended a flurry of official condolences from Washington, D.C.

The Keiths dealt with Ozzie's death as best as they could. By the end of that horrific month of March, Bertha was able to write about her feelings. In a letter to Bricker, she thanked him for his "splendid" letter that "...really helped to ease the terrible grief of those first few days. It just doesn't seem possible that 'Ozzie' is not coming back. We felt that perhaps he had something to give to the world. He was so happy to have his little play given so much recognition here at home." Bertha quoted Ozzie's description of Bricker in a letter he wrote after he flew his first combat mission: "I sincerely think that there is no finer mind in the theater world than Herschel's. The man's theater philosophy is something beyond all ordinary understanding, and with confidence in him and belief in his methods and theories--a person cannot help but get a good fundamental knowledge of theater, and a strong foundation for a career in theater or radio."

No other information surrounding Ozzie's death would be forthcoming to the Keiths even though pilots who witnessed a crash or accident, filed reports once they returned to base. In Missing Air Crew Report # 7 and # 8, two identical reports, but with different personnel names, Lt. Robert Anderson and three other AAF personnel, three officers and one enlisted man, gave testimony to what they witnessed. These reports were not available to family members.

The description of the accident was brief:

> "Element was approaching the Wing assembly point and at 27(degrees) 00'N 141(degrees) 00'E at 25 0146Z, B-29 (A-45) was pulling into formation over B-29 (A-44). Either A-44 or A-45 moved the wrong way causing both planes to collide. A-44 broke into several pieces and fell flaming into the ocean. A-45 went up on wing in a 90(degree) bank with his 2 inboard engines dead, then he went down to the deck."

"In the meantime another B-29 (A-51) made a turn to remain in the area and when next seen, A-45 had struck water and was burning. B-29 A-51 searched the area from 25 0146Z to 25 0325Z at altitudes from 200 to 1000 feet. Debris such as oxygen bottles, two inflated life rafts, one single life raft were seen; but no survivors were seen."

"The weather at the time of collision was, ceiling and visibility unlimited. The altitude of the colliding aircraft was 1500 feet. No one was seen to bail out of either aircraft."

The report listed the personnel for each aircraft. For A-44, Ponderous Peg (aircraft #42-53431), it listed Ozzie and his crew. For A-45,(aircraft #42-24808) it listed Jack Barnes and his crew. One passenger was also listed for this aircraft. Twenty-three airmen perished within a few minutes. On April 19, Lt Anderson and the three other witnesses who were in A-51, were rammed by a Japanese fighter during a bombing mission over Kyushu, Japan, and were lost.

Steve Birdsall, in his landmark book on the B-29, *Saga of the Superfortress,* described the collision as: "Ponderous Peg's luck finally ran out on February 25. At fifteen hundred feet, in perfectly clear conditions, another B-29 crashed into her from slightly above and behind. Ponderous Peg appeared to disintegrate and crashed to the water, exploding and sinking almost immediately. The other B-29 appeared to recover momentarily, then it too went down. Both crews were lost."

The Army Air Force assigned no blame for the collision. Indeed, a mid-air collision during WWII was an all too common an occurrence. More than 15,000 young airmen were lost either in collisions or other accidents. Brian Bell, retired United States Air Force officer, graduate of the Air Force Academy, pilot, and graduate of the University of Southern California Aircraft Accident Investigation course speculated recently on what may have happened. In his opinion, Aircraft 45 flown by Lt. Barnes was 'rejoining' (moving into formation) too high and too fast. Rejoining a formation is best from below so as to maintain visual contact with the aircraft in front of them. Should the aircraft in the front, Ponderous Peg, suddenly hit an air pocket or experience wind turbulence, the rejoining aircraft would have had time to react appropriately. Large, heavily bomb laden aircraft react slowly to erratic flying conditions.

The two inboard engines of Barnes's A-45 were dead after the collision according to the official report. These props may have chopped Ponderous Peg into pieces as it came down on top of it. (The B-29 was equipped with four massive four blade propellers to give it added lift to carry the necessary bomb load.) In addition to A-45's damaged engines, its control surfaces may also have been damaged to the extent that Barnes could not recover flight characteristics in time to avoid hitting the ocean although he valiantly tried to do so.

More information on those last moments for Ozzie may have brought some solace to the Keiths. As late as 1953, Bertha still sought more details. Her half-brother in Caribou, Sterling Tibbetts, encountered a Sgt. Hawkins, stationed at Loring Air Force Base, who claimed that he knew of the crash from his WWII service in the Marianas. In a moving letter never sent to a Sgt. Hawkins, Bertha, in a motherly way, requested information: "So many things have puzzled us such as just where it happened. How close to the Japanese mainland? Were there islands in the vicinity on which a possible survivor could have reached haven?...Was there any opportunity for bailing out?...We did wonder why the report was 'killed in action' instead of 'missing' as presumably no one could actually be sure there were no survivors--it being difficult to spot anything as small as a head from a fairly high altitude." Bertha acknowledged that the loss of, "Our only son, Austin, eight years ago...was a terrific shock to us..." But the Keiths would never know what really happened that February morning when those two B-29s collided. Indeed, only God knows what happened and what Ozzie and his crew and likewise Barnes and his crew experienced in those final moments.

The Keiths moved from Boynton Street to Norway Road in early 1946. Perhaps, Ozzie was too present in the old home. Marion went on to the University of Maine. Edgar continued to run his businesses, and Bertha resumed her community service activities. In 1947, Bertha was appointed Chairman of the Individual Subscriptions Division of the War Memorial Building fund drive. She said of this appointment: "I am one of the mothers in Bangor and throughout the country whose son did not come home from war. I feel that he and his comrades would be proud of this War Memorial Building. I know that he and the others would want a living memorial that will serve the community he loved and he youngsters growing up in it....All of us shared in the war effort and, as neighbors, we will see that the sacrifices of our sons and daughters will not be forgotten."

After just a few more years, the family moved to Hampden Highlands where Edgar tried his hand at running a nursery. Marion married in 1956, was divorced in 1961, and had no children. In 1957, the Keiths left Bangor and moved to Laconia, New Hampshire. They bought a small house on the shores of Lake Winnipesaukee and lived out their days there. Marion soon joined them but never remarried. All are gone now; no immediate family remains.

Epilogue

> "Those who have enjoyed such privileges as we enjoy forget in time that men have died to win them."
>
> Franklin Delano Roosevelt

Everyday, the turmoil and tumult that World War II brought to many homes and families of the 1940s fades further into collective American subconsciousness. For the Keiths, the impact of that cataclysmic world event was real. Their son, Ozzie, like so many of that generation, rose up in response to the call of his country. Citizen first, then soldier, Ozzie deferred his dreams of theater to the military exigencies of his time. Talented and personable, even lovable, sensitive and passionate, responsible and conscientious, Ozzie desperately wanted an acting career. Within his inner being, his passion for theater conflicted with the constraints of the military; theater was creative and expressive, the military was authoritative and rigid. He worried about having courage in the throes of fear. Yet, he needed to prove to himself that he could be a good soldier leading men into battle confidently and assuredly. Ozzie wanted to do what he saw as his patriotic duty.

Ozzie's greatest threat to achieving his life's dream was his own death in war; more and more he worried about this. His life situation was exacerbated when he arrived in the Marianas. Here, death lingered nearby. Yet in his own mind, two years earlier he had worked out some sense, logic, reason, purpose, and way to deal with the confused world at war he saw around him. He turned to God, and developed an unshakable trust in Him. He believed that whatever it might

Last Time Home, Summer 1944

Epilogue

mean for him personally, God directed all things. He accepted this, and it became his faith giving him the bravery to deal with the possible. This faith gave him the courage to fly into battle.

Fear of death in battle is not an uncommon emotion for a warrior. What is uncommon, is the ability to eloquently express this universal emotion with sincerity. Ozzie used a theatrical convention to express this emotion and his faith not only to others but for himself as well with his play, *Prelude to Courage*. The play is highly autobiographical for when Ozzie describes Johnny Emerson, he describes himself. When Ozzie sketches out the turmoil and conflict within the heart and mind of Steve Brown, he depicts his own internal conflict.

Ozzie, the dreamer, would not return after the war to his hometown on the banks of the Penobscot nor would he pick up where he left off at the Maine Masque and again work with the mentor he loved. Ozzie would never have his name on a theater marque, his greatest dream. That was the price of war. Yet he would always be remembered. "We feel that our lives have been blessed with something fine and beautiful in having been privileged to be Austin's parents," his mother wrote to Charles Crossland. The Reverend Frederick M. Meek, former Pastor of All Souls Congregational Church in Bangor and former pastor to the Keiths may have said it best:

> "Always know that Austin, that fine, clean, courageous boy, still goes on--living, clear-eyed as usual --developing, growing still in character and wisdom-- and occasionally waving a beckoning hand of encouragement to you all. I look forward to seeing him again--even as you shall do."

In 1948, Ozzie's aunt Pearl Tibbetts wrote a commemorative poem expressing the family's heart felt sentiments:

"Once There Was a Little Boy"

One of all God's many blessings,
As we've gone along life's way,
Was a chubby little boy
To love and cherish day by day.
Just a busy little boy
Taking mother's don'ts and do's,
Climbing trees and tearing trousers,
Coming home with muddy shoes.

He dug tunnels in the back yard,
Brought home snakes and such things too;
At times he tried Mom's patience,
The outlandish things he'd do.
Just a lively little fellow,
Wanting everything to try,
Winning hearts and being friendly,
Being "just a regular guy."

While he was just a tiny lad,
He loved to play a part;
"Once there was a little boy",
His stories all must start.
At twelve he had a paper route,
And in a contest, he--
By subscription-selling won first prize,
A trip to Washington D.C.

Dreaming dreams and drawing pictures,
Writing parodies on song,

Epilogue

He kept his teachers worried;
They thought he'd never get along.
Skits and programs for assembly
Was another specialty,
He loved everything in drama,
From leading role to scenery.

He did a lot of other things
That most all boys do,
Like swimming, skating, dancing,
And golf and bowling too.
He was in his seventh heaven
When he could act and sing;
If he wasn't doing Jolson
He was imitating Bing.

Sometimes An Old Cowhand,
Was the part he'd choose to do;
Chevalier was another,
Barrymore and Gable too.
In High he proved himself an actor,
By the praises he did win,
The time he really did his stuff
As Huckleberry Finn.

At U. of M. he joined The Masque,
Took part in all their plays,
Also with his Beta brothers
Spent many happy days.
He left his Alma Mater,
Home and friends and other things,
To join the Army Air Corps;
And he won his silver wings.

Clay modeling, painting, sketching,
Took up his leisure time;
While winning First Lieutenant bars,
He'd compose some verse or rhyme.
And then he'd write a story
To help fill up each day,
He won state-wide attention
On a little one-act play.

He was editor of *Propwash*,
And *Luke Field* graduation book--
Then camp radio announcer;
Must be he had what it took.
If he had an idle minute
He was planning something new,
It seemed that he was happiest,
With a dozen things to do.

He instructed fliers out at Merced
On single-engine planes,
Then went on to Super Bombers,
To go out to combat lanes.
He flew his plane across the sea,
Put his crew down on Saipan;
From there he flew his missions
To the mainland of Japan.

He'd pray for faith and courage
As they started on each flight;
And should God see fit to take him,
He'd never doubt that it was right.
Far across the blue Pacific
There's a sacred little place

Epilogue

Where in dreams we can imagine
That we see his smiling face.

Once in school he wrote a story
Of a rocket ship to Mars,
Did he know he'd fly a <u>Superfort</u>
'Way up among the stars?
Perhaps he saw the angels
As he was flying high;
Could he have gone to meet them
From his <u>Cabin In The Sky</u>?

Fond memories come back to us
To take away the hurt;
We'd tell him, " Keep those shoulders back."
And he'd say "It's just my shirt."
The time Pop took him hunting
Along some trail or creek,
And he came home with a story
About a "Little Squeak".

Then they'd have some boxing
And he didn't do so bad,
But knew he'd have to be a man
'Fore he could lick his dad.
Mom was a busy person,
Keeping both these boys in check,
For when they started playing,
It seemed like the house they'd wreck.

Just our own little <u>G.I. Joe</u>
He was proud that he could be

One of many million kids who fought
To keep our country free.
Though it's lonely here without him,
We'll carry on in pride and joy,
For life has been much sweeter,
Cause "Once There Was A Little Boy".

Today, somewhere in the depths of the Pacific lie the remains of A-44 and A-45. Amidst the charred and tangled debris of crews and crafts is a ring given so long ago by one Maine Masquer to another--a symbol of the past and a sign for the future. "Is this what became of us?" Not so for Ozzie for he saw beyond this world.

Notes

Chapter One

Page 1-John Ciardi in his wartime diary *Saipan* describes a day for a B-29 crew on a bombing mission. John Ciardi, *Saipan-The War Diary of John Ciardi* (Fayetteville:The University of Arkansas Press, 1988),38-43.

Page 2-Wesley Frank Craven and James Lea Cate, *The Army Air Forces in World War II* Volume 5.(Chicago: The University of Chicago Press, 1953), 572.

Page 2- Austin R. Keith to Herschel L. Bricker, 5 February 1945, Bricker Collection, Special Collections, The University of Maine.

Page 2- Curtis E. LeMay, *Mission with LeMay: My Story* (Garden City: Doubleday and Company, Inc., 1965), 4.

Page 3-Craven, p.571.

Page-3 Austin R. Keith to Herschel L. Bricker, 22 December 1944, Bricker Collection, Special Collections, The University of Maine.

Page 3-Kenneth P. Werrell, *Blankets of Fire* (Washington: Smithsonian Institution Press, 1996), 238.

Page 3-Steve Birdsall, *Saga of the Superfortress* (Garden City: Doubleday and Company, Inc. 1980), 25.

Page 4- Robert F. Dorr, *B-29, Superfortress Units of World War 2* (Oxford: Osprey Publishing, 2002) 13.

Page 4-*Fort Wayne Journal*, 7 March 1945, 1.

Page 4-Danville World War II Soldiers File, Danville Public Library, Danville, Illinois.

Page 5- e-mail notes from Dr. Peter Seel, Sgt. Seel's nephew, October 23, 2009.

Page 5- Dorr, 13.

Page 5- Werrell, *Blankets of Fire*, xi.

Page 5-Austin R. Keith to Herschel L. Bricker, 3 September 1944, Bricker Collection, Special Collections, The University of Maine.

Page 6- *Daily Courier,* March 2, 1945, 1.

Page 6-*Alexandria Gazette,* March 24, 1945, 1.

Page 6-*Butler Eagle,* March 2, 1945, 1.

Page 6- *Amsterdam Recorder,* April 19, 1945, 1.

Page 7- Birdsall, 6-7, 22-23.

Page 7- *Rochester Democrat and Chronicle,* March 13, 1945,1.

Page 7- Austin R. Keith to Herschel L. Bricker, 3 September 1944, Bricker Collection, Special Collections, The University of Maine.

Page 7- *New Haven Register,* March 12, 1945, 1.

Page 7-Dorr,14.

Page 8- *Pottsville Republican,* March 5, 1945, 1.

Page 8-Austin R. Keith to Herchel L. Bricker, 3 September 1944, Bricker Collection, The University of Maine.

Page 8- Austin R. Keith to Herchel L.Bricker, 15 January 1945, Bricker Collection, Special Collections, The University of Maine.

Page 9- Toki Takai and Henry Sakaida, *Hunters of the* JAAF(Oxford:Osprey Publishing,2001),122-123.

Page 10- Birdsall, 147, 157.

Page 10- Birdsall, 128-133.

Chapter Two

Page 11-Bertha Keith kept two baby books that detail Austin's first years: one is entitled "The Best Baby published by Borden Eagle Brand, and "Our Baby", publisher unknown.

Page 12-Memorandum booklet kept by Bertha Keith.

Page 12-Mrs. Jane Knight, telephone conversation with the author, 20 April 2009.

Notes

Page 13- "Washington Trip Winner Prepares To Visit Capital," *Bangor Daily News*, 23 December 1931, 2.

Page 13-Pearl M.Tibbetts, "Once There Was a Little Boy," a poem, 1948.

Page 14- Mrs. Bette Barker Taverner, telephone conversation with the author, 11 November 2009.

Page 15- Bangor High School literary magazine, *Oracle* (February 1936) 8, 9, 32.

Page 15-16- Bangor High School literary magazine, *Oracle* (December 1936) 11, 12, 38.

Page 17- Bangor High School literary magazine, *Oracle* (March 1937) 13, 14, 32, 34, 36.

Page 17-"B.H.S. Dramatic Club Stages 'Tom Sawyer'," *Bangor Daily News*, 12 December 1936, p. 13.

Page 17-"Bangor H.S. Class Stages 'Skidding'," *Bangor Daily News*, 22 May 1937, p. 13.

Page 18-"Bangor R.O.T.C. Units in Annual Review Friday," *Bangor Daily News*, 29 may 1937, 1.

Page 18- Bangor High School literary magazine, *Oracle* (March 1938) 7, 8, 34, 36.

Page 19-Mrs. Bette Barker Taverner, letter to the author, August 4, 2009.

Page 19-Mrs. Better Barker Taverner, telephone conversation with the author, 9 September 2009.

Page 19-*Bangor City Directories*, (Springfield, MA, H.A. Manning Co., 1930-1940).

Page 19-Mrs. Jane Knight, telephone conversations with the author, 20 April 2009 and 7 July 2009.

Page 20- "CMTC Battalion Commanders and Aides," *Bangor Daily News*, 15 July 1938, 5.

Page 20- Bette Barker Taverner, letter to the author, 4 August 2009.

Page 20- Tibbetts.

Page 20-Obituaries, *Bangor Daily News*, 3 December 2002, p. 15.

Page 20-Charles D. Bartlett, Jr. Letter to Edgar and Bertha Keith, 12 April 1945.

Page 20-Memorandum booklet.

Page 21-Ralph O. Brewster, U. S. Congressman, letter to Austin R. Keith, 18 January 1940.

Chapter Three

Page 22-Stephen L. Jacobs,*The Class of 1944 in World War II* (Orono, The University Alumni Association, 2001) 3.

Page 23-Marion Cooper, "Maine Masque Theatre Does Fine Work in Modern Play Production," *Lewiston Journal Magazine Section*, 21 April 1945, 1.

Page 24-Herschel L. Bricker *Student (Questionnaire) Sheet*, Bricker Collection, Special Collections, The University of Maine.

Page 24-"'Masque' Prepares Two Years for 'Hamlet'," *The Maine Campus*, 6 March 1941, 1.

Page 25-Walter R. Whitney, "Little Theatre Inadequate As Packed Houses View 'Hamlet'," *The Maine Campus*, 13 March 1941, 1,4.

Page 25-*Maine Masque Makes "Good Show" of Its Uncut Version of "Hamlet"*, Bangor Daily News, 11 March 1941, 5.

Page 25-"'Masque' Gives Benefit Show," *The Maine Campus*, 20 March 1941, 1.

Page 25-Herschel L. Bricker, Unpublished Autobiography, Special Collections, The University of Maine.

Page 26-Handout produced by Keith and Brown, 15 May 1941, Bricker Collection, Special Collections, The University of Maine.

Page 26-*Masque To Stage 'Ah Wilderness!',*The Maine Campus, 10 April 1941, 1.

Notes

Page 26-Oscar Shepard, "Maine Masque Present Play by Eugene O'Neill," *Bangor Daily News*, 29 April 1941, 5.

Page 27-"Maine Masque Closes Successful Season-Austin Keith Takes Acting Honors in 'Ah, Wilderness'" *The Maine Campus*, 1 May 1941, 1.

Page 28-Directory, *The Maine Campus*, 2 October 1941, 2.

Page 28-"The Golden Apple,"*The Maine Campus*, 2 October 1941, 1.

Page 28-"Maine Masque Scores Hit in Original Musical Comedy,"*Bangor Daily News*, 4 November 1941, 5.

Page 28-29-Milton Ellis, "Review of the Acting Class Performance of Saroyan's *Jim Dandy*," December 1941, Unpublished manuscript, Bricker Collection, Special Collections, The University of Maine.

Page 29-30-Herschel L. Bricker, "Chapter V, Theatre in Wartime," Unpublished Autobiography, The Bricker Collection, The University of Maine.

Page 30-Bangor Service Record, Bangor Public Library, 1946.

Page 30- World War II Army Enlistment Records, U. S. National Archives and Records Administration, aad.archives.gov

Chapter Four

Page 31- Much of the information for this chapter comes from letters written by Austin Keith to Professor Bricker. The letters are dated April 17, 1942 to January 10, 1943 and are contained in the Bricker Collection, Special Collections, The University of Maine. When direct quotation is used, the author cites specific letters by date within the text. Other documents used in the chapter are cited as appropriate.

Page 31-Austin R. Keith file, The Bangor Room, Bangor Public Library.

Page 32-33-Twenty third birthday card to Austin Keith from his parents, April 13, 1942, author's collection.

Page 32- Austin R. Keith, letter to Herschel Bricker, May 29, 1942.

Page 33- Earle Rankin, Letter to Herschel Bricker, June 8, 1942, Bricker Collection, Special Collections, The University of Maine.

Page 33-Austin Rodney Keith, undated letter to Gwen Cushing, author's collection.

Page 33-Gwen Cushing, letter to Herschel Bricker, June 12, 1942, Bricker Collection, Special Collections, The University of Maine.

Page 34-National Museum of the US Air Force, www.nationalmuseum.af.mil/factsheets/factsheet.asp?id=479

Page 34-Austin Rodney Keith, letter to Herschel Bricker, June 25, 1942.

Page 35-Austin R. Keith, Ed. *Prop Wash Class of 42-K*, Sequoia Field, July 26, 1942.

Page 35-*Jane's Fighting Aircraft of World War II*(London:The Random House Group Ltd.,1989), p. 219.

Page 35-Austin R. Keith, letter to Herschel Bricker, September 11, 1942.

Page 36- Austin R. Keith, letter to Herschel Bricker, September 27, 1942.

Page 36-Austin R. Keith, letter to Herschel Bricker, October 12, 1942.

Page 37-Jane's, p. 251.

Page 38-40-Austin R. Keith, Editor, *Luke Field, Class 42-K*, Phoenix Engraving and Lithographing Company, 1942.

Page 40-41- Austin R. Keith, letter to Herschel Bricker, November 23, 1942.

Page 41-Luke Field 42-K Yearbook.

Page 41-Austin R. Keith, letter to Herschel Bricker, December 14, 1942.

Page 42-Austin R. Keith, letter to Herschel Bricker, February 2, 1943.

Chapter Five

Page 30-Much of the information for this chapter comes from letters written by Austin Keith to Professor Bricker. The letters are dated 11 January 1943 to 9 March 1944 and are contained in the Bricker Collection, Special Collections, The University of Maine. When direct quotation is

Notes 129

used, the author cites specific letters by date within the text. Other documents used in the chapter are cited as appropriate.

Page 44-Austin R. Keith Alumni File, Special Collections, The University of Maine.

Page 45-Knight.

Page 45-The Baptismal Font (New York: Abingdon-Cokesbury Press, 1940).

Page 46-Jane's, 206.

Page 46-47-Norman Mennes letter to Herschel Bricker, July 21, 1943, Bricker Collection, Special Collections, The University of Maine.

Page 46-Earle Rankin letter to Herschel Bricker, Bricker Collection, The University of Maine, August 19, 1943.

Page 48-Earle Rankin letter to Herschel Bricker, October 28, 1943.

Chapter Seven

Page 66-Much of the information for this chapter comes from letters written by Austin Keith to Professor Bricker. The letters are dated 30 March 1944 to 17 December 1944 and are contained in the Bricker Collection, Special Collections, The University of Maine. When direct quotation is used, the author cites specific letters by date within the text. Other documents used in the chapter are cited as appropriate.

Page 67-General Henry H. Arnold Letter to All Aviation Trainees from Army Service Forces and Army Ground Forces, April 1, 1944, Bricker Collection, Special Collections, The University of Maine.

Page 67-Wesley F. Craven and James L., Cate *The Army Air Forces in World War II, Volume Six* (Chicago: The University of Chicago Press, 1955), 607.

Page 68-Maine Masque Theatre Playwriting Contest guidelines, Bricker Collection, Special Collections, The University of Maine.

Page 69-Jane's, pp.209-210.

Page 69-Army Air Forces Pilot School Diploma, 3 June 1944, author's collection.

Page 70-Craven, 607-608.

Page 70-The Maine Masque Newsletter, Vol.II, July 1, 1944, Bricker Collection, Special Collections, The University of Maine.

Page 71-Craven, p. 628.

Page 72- C.B. Dear, Editor *The Oxford Guide -World War II* (Oxford, Oxford University Press, 1995),758,759.

Page 73- Audrey Coster, letter to Mr. and Mrs. Keith, 4 April 1945.

Page 76-Editorial, *The Maine Campus*, November 2, 1944, 2.

Page 78-"Young Bangor Aviator Develops Literary Skill; Writes Little Play," *Bangor Daily News*, February 10, 1945.

Page 79-Craven, 605, 606.

Page 79-80-Linda McCaffery *The History of the B-29 Superfortress* Text of the Plaques at the B-29 Memorial Formerly the Great Bend Army Air Field, Great Bend, Kansas, (pdf document:http://paaf.indexks.com), 6.

Page 80-Craven, 595.

Page 80-Curtis LeMay, *Superfortress* (Yardley, Westhome, 2006), 46.

Chapter Eight

Page 83-85-Austin R. Keith to Herschel L. Bricker, 22 December 1944, Bricker Collection, Special Collections, The University of Maine.

Page 85-Francis H. Roth Jr. to Edgar and Bertha Keith, 23 March 1945, Author's Collection.

Page 85-Earle A. Rankin to Herschel L. Bricker, 27 December 1944, Bricker Collection, Special Collections, The University of Maine.

Page 86-Earle A Rankin to Herschel L. Bricker, 4 January 1945, Bricker Collection, Special Collections, The University of Maine.

Page 86-Last Will and Testament of Austin R Keith, 4 January 1945, Author's Collection.

Page 86-Austin R. Keith to Herschel L. Bricker, 8 January 1945, Bricker Collection, Special Collections, The University of Maine.

Page 87- Austin R. Keith to Herschel L. Bricker, 15 January 1945, Bricker Collection, Special Collections, The University of Maine.

Page 88- Austin R. Keith to Herschel L. Bricker, 23 January 1944, Bricker Collection, Special Collections, The University of Maine.

Page 88-Austin R. Keith to Charles E. Crossland, 18 January 1945, Alumni Files, Special Collections, The University of Maine.

Page 88-Charles E. Crossland to Austin R. Keith, 31 January 1945, Alumni Files, Special Collections, The University of Maine.

Page 88-Austin R. Keith to Herschel L. Bricker, February 5, 1945, Bricker Collection, Special Collections, The University of Maine.

Page 89-John Ciardi, *Saipan* (Fayetteville, The University of Arkansas Press, 1988)100.

Page 90-93- Austin R. Keith to his parents, 28 January 1945, Author's Collection.

Page 92- Austin spells "dying" as "dieing".

Chapter Nine

Page 94-Wilfred M. Lind, " With a B-29 Over Japan-A Pilot's Story," *The New York Times Magazine*, 25 March 1945, 6.

Page 95-Lind, 38.

Page 96-Earle A. Rankin letter to Herschel Bricker, March 7, 1945, Bricker Collection, Special Collections, The University of Maine.

Page 96-Lt. Colonel Frank L. Davis letter to Mr. Edgar Keith, March 14, 1945, Author's Collection.

Page 96-Dennis M. Savage, *B-29 Superfortress-Walk Around* (Carrollton:

Squadron/Signal Publications, 2008), 49.

Page-97 Savage, 36.

Page-97 Savage, 59.

Page-98 Ciardi, 60.

Page-98 *Service Book and Hymnal*, Lutheran Churches, 1958, 576.

Chapter Ten

Page 99-*Bangor Daily News*, March 2, 1945, 1.

Page 99- *Bangor Daily News*, 11.

Page 100- G. Scott Gorman, *Endgame in the Pacific* (Maxwell Air Force Base, Alabama: Fairchild Paper, 2000), 49.

Page 100-*Bangor Daily News*, 3-4 March, 1945, 2.

Page 101-Mrs. Jane Knight, telephone conversation with the author, 23 March 2010 and 20 April 2009.

Page 102-*Bangor Daily News*, 3-4 March, 1945, 5.

Page 102-103-Letter to Edgar and Bertha Keith from Herschel L. Bricker, March 2, 1945, Author's Collection.

Page 103-Letter to Herschel L. Bricker from Annie Barr, March 31, 1945, Bricker Collection Special Collections, The University of Maine.

Page 103-Letter to Herschel L. Bricker from Marion Cooper, March 26, 1945, Bricker Collection, Special Collections, The University of Maine.

Page 103-"Maine Masque Theatre Does Fine Work in Modern Play Production," *Lewiston Journal*, April 21, 1945, 4.

Page 103-"Lt. Austin Keith Superfort Pilot Lost in Action,"*Bangor Daily News*,3-4 March, 1945, 1.

Page-103- Bertha Keith's log book, Author's Collection.

Page 103-104-Letter to Edgar and Bertha Keith from Charles D. Bartlett,

Notes

Jr. April 12, 1945, Author's Collection.

Page 104-Letter to Edgar and Bertha Keith from Francis H. Roth, Jr., March 23, 1945, Author's Collection.

Page 104-Letter to Edgar and Bertha Keith from Webber J. Mason, May 24, 1945, Author's Collection.

Page 104-105-Letter to Herschel L. Bricker from Maynard French, March 8, 1945, Bricker Collection, Special Collections, The University of Maine.

Page 105-Letter to Herschel L. Bricker from William S. Brown, April 14, 1945, Bricker Collection, Special Collections, The University of Maine.

Page 105- "For Ozzie" a poem by Norman Mennes, April 16, 1945, Author's Collection.

Page 105-106-Editorial, *The Maine Campus*, March 8, 1945, 2.

Page 106- Letter to Edgar and Bertha Keith from Manning Hawthorne, March 5, 1945, Author's Collection.

Page 106-Letter to Edgar and Bertha Keith from Arthur A. Hauck, March 7, 1945, Author's Collection.

Page 107-108-Letter to Herschel L. Bricker from Earle A. Rankin, March 7, 1945, Bricker Collection, The University of Maine.

Page 108-Letter to Mr. Edgar Keith from Major E. A. Bradunas, Assistant Chief of Air Staff, Personnel, Headquarters, Army Air Forces, March 13, 1945, Author's Collection.

Page 108-109- Letter to Mr. Edgar Keith from Lt. Colonel Frank. Davis, Commander of the 871st Bombardment Squadron, March 14, 1945, Author's Collection.

Page 109-110- Card to Mr. Edgar Keith from General Marshall, Chief of Staff, U.S. Army, Author's Collection.

Page 110-Letter to Mr. Edgar Keith from Lt. General Barney M. Giles, Deputy Commander, Army Air Forces and Chief of Staff, April 2, 1945, Author's Collection.

Page 110-Letter to Mr. Edgar Keith from Henry L. Stimson, Secretary of

War, April 3, 1945, Author's Collection.

Page 110-Letter to Mr. Edgar Keith from H.H.Arnold, Commanding General, Army Air Forces Memorial Day, 1945, Author's Collection.

Page 111- Letter to Herschel L. Bricker from Bertha Keith, March 21, 1945, Bricker The Bricker Collection, Special Collections, The University of Maine.

Page111-112-Missing Air Crew Report # 7(12722) and # 8 (12721)Department of the Air Force, Air Force Historical Research Agency (AFHRA), Maxwell Air Force Base, Alabama.

Page 111-112-Time(Zulu) and location (longitude and latitude) are consistent with military usage. The term "deck" refers to ocean surface.

Page112-*The Long Haul, The Story of the 497th Bomb Group(VH)* (Newsfoto Publishing Co, 1947) Chapter XV.

Page 112- Birdsall, 133.

Page 112-e-mail notes from Brian Bell, July 23, 2009, July 24, 2009, and April 2, 2010.

Page 113-114-Uncompleted letter to Sgt. Hawkins from Bertha Tibbetts, 1953, Author's Collection.

Page 114-"Gold Star Mother Heads Memorial Division of Drive," *Bangor Daily News,* May 31-June 1, 1947, 11. This building in Bangor was never built.

Epilogue

Page 117-Letter to Charles E. Crossland, Executive Secretary, University of Maine Alumni Association from Bertha Keith, May 29, 1945, Alumni File, Special Collections, The University of Maine.

Page 117-Letter to Edgar Keith from Rev. Frederick M. Meek, D.D., April 18, 1945, Author's Collection.

Page 118-122-"Once There Was a Little Boy", Poem by Pearl Tibbetts, Author's Collection.

Bibliography

Bangor High School *Oracle*.(February 1936): 8,9,32.

Bangor High School *Oracle* (December 1936): 11,12,38.

Bangor High School *Oracle* (March 1937):13,14,32,34,36.

Birdsall, Steve. *Saga of the Superfortress*. Garden City: Doubleday and Company, Inc., 1980.

Bricker, Herschel L. Papers and Letters. The University of Maine Library

Ciardi, John . *Saipan-The War Diary of John Ciardi*. Fayetteville: The University of Arkansas Press, 1988.

Cooper, Marion. "Maine Masque Theatre Does Fine Work in Modern Play Production." *Lewiston Journal Magazine* (21 April, 1945): 1.

Craven,Wesley Frank and James Lea Cate. *The Army Air Forces in World War II*. Chicago: The University of Chicago Press, 1953.

Dear, C.B. ed. *The Oxford Guide-World War II*. Oxford: Oxford University Press, 1995.

Dorr, Robert F. *B-29, Superfortress Units of World War 2*. Oxford: Osprey Publishing, 2002.

Ellis, Milton. "Review of the Acting Class Performance of Saroyan's *Jim Dandy*." Bricker Collection, The University of Maine.

Gorman, G. Scott. *Endgame in the Pacific-Complexity, Strategy, and the B-29*. Maxwell Air Force Base: Air Unversity Press, 2000.

Hansell Jr., Haywood S. *Strategic Air War Against Japan*. Washington: U. S. Government Printing Office, 1980.

Jacobs, Stephen L. *The Class of 1944 in World War II*. Orono: The University Alumni Association, 2001.

Jablonski, Edward. *Airwar*. Garden City, Doubleday and Company, Inc., 1971.

Jane's Fighting Aircraft of World War II London: The Random House Group Ltd., 1989.

Johnson, Arnold T. *The Long Haul-The Story of the 497th Bomb Group.* San Angelo: Newsfoto Publishing Company, 1947.

Keith, Austin R. ed. *Prop Wash Class of 42-K.* Visalia: Sequoia Field, 1942.

Keith, Austin R. ed. *Luke Field, Class 42-K.* Phoenix: Phoenix Engraving and Lithographing Company, 1942.

LeMay, Curtis E. *Mission with LeMay: My Story.* Garden City: Doubleday and Company, Inc., 1965.

LeMay, Curtis E. *Superfortress.* Yardley: Westholme Publishing, LLC, 2006.

Lind, Wilfred M. "With a B-29 Over Japan-A Pilot's Story." *The New York Times Magazine,* (25 March 1945):5-8.

McCaffery, Linda. *The History of B-29 Superfortress.* Great Bend: Great Bend Army Air Field, 2011.

O'Donnell, Emmett. *The Story of the 73rd-The Unofficial History of the 73rd Bomb Wing.* San Antonio: Newsome Publishing Company, 1946.

Pyle, Ernie *Last Chapter.* New York: Henry Holt and Company, 1945.

Savage, Dennis M. *B-29 Superfortress-Walk Around.* Carrolton: Squadron/Signal Publications, 2008.

Shepard, Oscar. "Maine Masque Presents Play by Eugene O'Neill ." *The Bangor Daily News* (29 April, 1941):1.

Takai, Toki and Henry Sakaida . *Hunters of the JAAF.* Oxford:Osprey Publishing, 2001.

U. S. National Archives and Records Administration. *World War II Army Enlistment Records.* aad.archives.gov

Werrell, Kenneth *Blankets of Fire.* Washington: Smithsonian Institution Press, 1996.

Whitney, Walter R. "Little Theatre Inadequate as Packed Houses View 'Hamlet'." *The Maine Campus* (11 March 1941):5.

Index

Ah Wilderness, 26
Air Corps Replacement Training Center (Anta Ana), 31
American Harvard AT-6, 37
AN/APQ-13 radar, 7
Anderson, Lieutenant Robert J. 95, 98, 111, 112
Army Reserve officer Training Corps, 14
Arnold, General Henry H., 2, 67, 110

Bailee, Reverend Arlan, 101
Bangor High Drama Club, 77
Bangor High School, 14
Bangor, Maine, 10, 11, 69
Bangor Public Library, 102
Barker (Taverner), Bette, 14, 18, 19, 29
Barry, Eugene, 6-7, 80, 97
Bartlett, Jr., Charles, 20, 103-104
Barnes, Lieutenant Jack S., 95, 98, 112
Beechcraft AT-11, 46
Bell, Brian, 113
Beta Theta Pi, 27
Blakely, Reverend Harold, 45
Boeing B-17, 5, 6, 66, 79
Boeing B-29 Superfortress, 1, 3, 5, 6, 67-69, 71, 79, 86
Bombardment Group, 497th, 3, 83, 108
Bonin Islands, 1, 94
Bowlaway, The, 19, 100
Bradunas, Major E. A. 108
Bricker, Herschel L., 6, 23, 24, 25, 26, 28, 33, 35, 36, 40, 42, 43, 44, 45, 46, 47, 49, 50, 51, 66, 68, 69, 70, 72, 73, 74, 75, 76, 77, 78, 80, 81, 84, 85, 86, 87, 88, 89, 102-104, 104, 106, 107, 111

Broitzman, Flight Officer, 5-6 79, 96-97
Brown, William, 25-26, 105
Bunga, Lieutenant James B., 1, 8, 80

Carlsbad, New Mexico, 45, 78, 83, 85
Caruso, Sergeant Liugi, 8, 80, 97, 98
Central Fire Control (CFC), 6
Chadwick, Lewis, 71
Citizens Military Training Camp, (CMTC), 20
Clovis Army Air Field, 6, 71, 74, 79, 83
Consolidated Vultee BT-13, 35
Coster, Audry, 73-74
Coster, Sergeant Lloyd H., 7, 73, 97
Crossland, Charles E., 44, 71, 88
Cushing, Gwen, 33

Davis, Colonel Frank L., 108-109
DeCourcy, Dayton, 71
Dow Field, 29, 78, 100
Dow, Lieutenant James F., 23
Dugan, Sergeant Charles R., 7, 80, 97

Electric Appliance Corporation, 19
Flick, Sergeant Robert C. 7, 80, 97
Formation Flying, 35, 95
French, Maynard, 48, 69, 104

Ghastly Goose, The, 9, 83, 86, 87, 95

Hamlet, 23, 25, 83

Hansell Jr., General Haywood S., 2
Hauck, Arthur A., 22, 44, 106
Hawthorne, Manning, 106
Helmke, Technical Sergeant
  Lawrence D., 4, 80, 97
Hobbs Army Air Field, 66, 85

Islely Field, 5, 10, 83, 87
Iwo Jima, 94, 99

Jim Dandy-Fat Man in a Famine,
  28-29

Johnston Island, 87

Katchmir, Lieutenant Wassil, 1, 8,
  10, 94, 95, 97-98
Kearney Army Air Field, 9, 80, 83
Keith, Austin Rodney (Ozzie)
  Airplane Commander B-29, 1, 10,
  110
  Birth, 12
  Childhood, 12-14
  High School, 14-21
  College Days, 22-30
  Flight Training
    Primary, 32-35
    Basic, 35-36
    Advanced, 36-41
  Training Command, 43-52
  Combat Preparation, 66-82
  Pacific Theater of Operations
    83-93
  New Play, 84-85
  Final Mission, 94-98
Keith (Tibbetts) Bertha U., 11, 100-
  101, 103, 110-111, 113, 114
Keith, Edgar N. 11, 19, 88, 99-100,
  114
Keith, Marion L., 12, 101, 114
Kwajalein Island, 87

Laconia ,New Hampshire, 114
LeMay, General Curtis, 2, 89
Lincoln Army Air Field, 69, 70
Luke Field, Class 42K Yearbook,
  37-40
Luke Field (The West Coast
  Training Center) 41

Maine Masque, 23,24, 48, 76
  78
Manhattan Project, 3
Marcoux, Nancy J., ix
Marshall, General George C.
  109
Mason, Weber, 104
Mather Field, 41, 86
Maxwell Field, 31
Meek, Reverend Frederick M.,
  117
Mennes, Norman, 33, 46-47,
  66, 105
Merced Army Flying School, 35,
  41, 43
Methodist Episcopal Church, 45
Missing Air Crew Reports
  (MACR), 111-112

Newpaper Boys Pilgrimage,, 13
New Sweden, Maine, 11
Norden Bomb Sight, 96

Oracle, 14-16

Pacific Theater of Operations
  (PTO), 87
Peterson, Captain Dale W. , 9, 95
Precision Bombing, 2
Prop Wash, 34
Ponderous Peg, 1, 2, 9-10, 94,
  95, 112

Index

Prelude to Courage
(One Act Play), 41, 52, 53-65, 70, 74-75, 76, 77, 102, 103

Rankin, Earle, 24, 29, 30, 33, 43, 48, 66, 75, 78, 80-82, 83, 85-86, 106-107
Rosenthal, Joseph, 99
Roth, Francis H. (Franny), 85, 104
Ryan PT-22 Recruit, 34

Saipan, 2, 72
Seel, Peter, 15
Seel, Sergeant William M., 5, 80, 97
Sequoia Field, 32
Skidding, 17
Smith, Jr., Lieutenant Milton E., 4, 73, 80, 87, 94, 97
Squadron, 871st, 109
Stimson, Secretary of War Henry L. 110

The Adventures of Tom Sawyer, 17
The Golden Apple, 28
The Maine Campus, 23, 76. 105
Tibbetts, Forrest, 11
Tibbetts, Pearl, 11, 19, 100, 101, Poem, 118-122
Tibbetts, Sterling, 113

Ulio, Major General J. A., 101, 110
University of Maine, 21, 22,
University of Maine Alumni Association, 88

Wing Assembly Area, 94, 96, 109
Wing, 73rd, 3
Wooster (Knight), Jane, 101

XX Air Force, 83
XXI Bomber Command, 2, 83

ABOUT THE AUTHOR

DAVID BERGQUIST lives and writes in Hermon, Maine following a career in higher education. With bachelor's and master's degrees from the University of Maine and a doctorate from the University of Nebraska, he served for thirty years as a college administrator. He is an avid historian and frequently writes and lectures about World War II history.

www.ingramcontent.com/pod-product-compliance
Lightning Source LLC
Chambersburg PA
CBHW071417160426
43195CB00013B/1720